Reach
HIGHER

Practice Book

Australia · Brazil · Mexico · Singapore · United Kingdom · United States

National Geographic Learning,
a Cengage Company

Reach Higher Practice Book 6B

Publisher, Content-based English: Erik Gundersen

Associate Director, R&D: Barnaby Pelter

Senior Development Editors:
   Jacqueline Eu
   Ranjini Fonseka
   Kelsey Zhang

Development Editor: Rayne Ngoi

Director of Global Marketing: Ian Martin

Heads of Regional Marketing:
   Charlotte Ellis (Europe, Middle East and Africa)
   Kiel Hamm (Asia)
   Irina Pereyra (Latin America)

Product Marketing Manager: David Spain

Senior Production Controller: Tan Jin Hock

Senior Media Researcher (Covers): Leila Hishmeh

Senior Designer: Lisa Trager

Director, Operations: Jason Seigel

Operations Support:
   Rebecca Barbush
   Drew Robertson
   Caroline Stephenson
   Nicholas Yeaton

Manufacturing Planner: Mary Beth Hennebury

Publishing Consultancy and Composition:
   MPS North America LLC

© 2020 Cengage Learning, Inc.

ALL RIGHTS RESERVED. No part of this work covered by the copyright herein may be reproduced or distributed in any form or by any means, except as permitted by U.S. copyright law, without the prior written permission of the copyright owner.

"National Geographic", "National Geographic Society" and the Yellow Border Design are registered trademarks of the National Geographic Society ® Marcas Registradas

For permission to use material from this text or product, submit all requests online at **cengage.com/permissions**
Further permissions questions can be emailed to
permissionrequest@cengage.com

ISBN-13: 978-0-357-36708-7

National Geographic Learning
200 Pier Four Blvd
Boston, MA 02210
USA

Locate your local office at **international.cengage.com/region**

Visit National Geographic Learning online at **ELTNGL.com**
Visit our corporate website at **www.cengage.com**

Printed in China
Print Number: 08   Print Year: 2023

Contents

Unit 5: A Time to Act

Part 1

Unit 5 Concept Map 5.1
Thinking Map: Main Idea Web 5.2
Grammar: Past Tense 5.3
Key Points Reading:
   "The Civil Rights Movement" 5.4
Grammar: Future Tense 5.5
Reread and Retell: Main Idea Web 5.6
Fluency: Intonation 5.7
Reading Options: Reflection Journal 5.8
Respond and Extend: Venn Diagram 5.9
Grammar: Verb Tenses 5.10
Close Reading: "Rosa Parks: My Story" 5.11

Part 2

Thinking Map: Theme Chart 5.14
Grammar: Present Perfect Tense 5.15
Key Points Reading: "Ayanna Sits In" 5.16
Grammar: Past and Future Perfect Tenses 5.17
Reread and Retell: Theme Chart 5.18
Fluency: Expression 5.19
Reading Options: Reflection Journal 5.20
Respond and Extend: Comparison Chart 5.21
Grammar: Perfect Tense Verbs 5.22
Close Reading:
   "Roll of Thunder, Hear My Cry" 5.23
Writing Project: Write an Argument 5.26

Unit 6: Food for Thought

Part 1

Unit 6 Concept Map 6.1
Thinking Map: Double Sequence Chain 6.2
Grammar: Pronoun Antecedents 6.3
Key Points Reading: "Seedfolks" 6.4
Grammar:
   Pronouns with Compound Antecedents 6.5
Vocabulary: Apply Word Knowledge 6.6
Reread and Retell:
   Double Sequence Chain 6.7
Fluency: Intonation 6.8
Reading Options: Dialogue Journal 6.9
Respond and Extend: Comparison Chart 6.10
Grammar: Pronouns 6.11
Close Reading: "Soul-Soothing Soups" 6.12

Part 2

Thinking Map: Argument Chart 6.15
Grammar:
   Indefinite and Demonstrative Pronouns 6.16
Key Points Reading: "The End of Plenty" 6.17
Grammar: Reflexive and
   Intensive Pronouns 6.19
Reread and Retell: Argument Chart 6.20
Fluency: Phrasing 6.21
Reading Options: Fact Cards 6.22
Respond and Extend: Comparison Chart 6.23
Grammar: Different Kinds of Pronouns 6.24
Close Reading: "How Altered?" 6.25
Writing Project: Write an Editorial 6.28

Unit 7: Ancient China

Part 1

Unit 7 Concept Map 7.1
Thinking Map: Text Evidence Chart. 7.2
Grammar: Vague Pronouns. 7.3
Key Points Reading:
 "The Emperor's Silent Army:
 Terracotta Warriors of Ancient China" 7.4
Grammar: Vague Pronouns. 7.6
Reread and Retell: Text Evidence Chart. 7.7
Fluency: Phrasing 7.8
Reading Options: Fact Cards 7.9
Respond and Extend:
 Comparison Chart 7.10
Grammar: Pronoun Agreement. 7.11
Close Reading: "A Silent Army" 7.12

Part 2

Thinking Map: Double Plot Diagram 7.15
Grammar:
 Prepositions and Prepositional Phrases 7.16
Key Points Reading:
 "Where the Mountain Meets the Moon" 7.17
Grammar: Expand Sentences
 with Prepositional Phrases 7.19
Vocabulary: Apply Word Knowledge 7.20
Reread and Retell: Double Plot Diagram 7.21
Fluency: Expression 7.22
Reading Options: Reflection Journal 7.23
Respond and Extend: Comparison Chart 7.24
Grammar: Prepositional Phrases 7.25
Close Reading: "Mu Lan:
 The Girl Who Knew No Fear" 7.26
Writing Project: Write a Narrative 7.29

Unit 8: Earth and Beyond

Part 1

Unit 8 Concept Map 8.1
Thinking Map: Comparison-Contrast Chart . . . 8.2
Grammar: Compound
 Sentences and Conjunctions 8.3
Key Points Reading:
 "Finding Mars on Earth" 8.4
Grammar: Complex Sentences 8.6
Reread and Retell:
 Comparison-Contrast Chart 8.7
Fluency: Intonation 8.8
Reading Options: Fact Cards 8.9
Respond and Extend: Comparison Chart 8.10
Grammar: Compound and
 Complex Sentences 8.11
Close Reading: "Here, There, and Beyond" 8.13

Part 2

Thinking Map: Word Choice Chart 8.16
Grammar: Combine Sentences 8.17
Key Points Reading:
 "Journey to the Center of the Earth" 8.18
Reread and Retell: Word Choice Chart 8.20
Fluency: Expression 8.21
Reading Options: K-W-L-Q Chart 8.22
Respond and Extend: Comparison Chart 8.23
Grammar: Combine Sentences 8.24
Close Reading: "Deep Into Darkness" 8.25
Writing Project:
 Write a Science Fiction Story 8.28
Photographic Credits 8.32

Name _____ Date _____

Unit Concept Map

A Time to Act

Make a concept map with the answers to the Big Question:
Why do people take a stand?

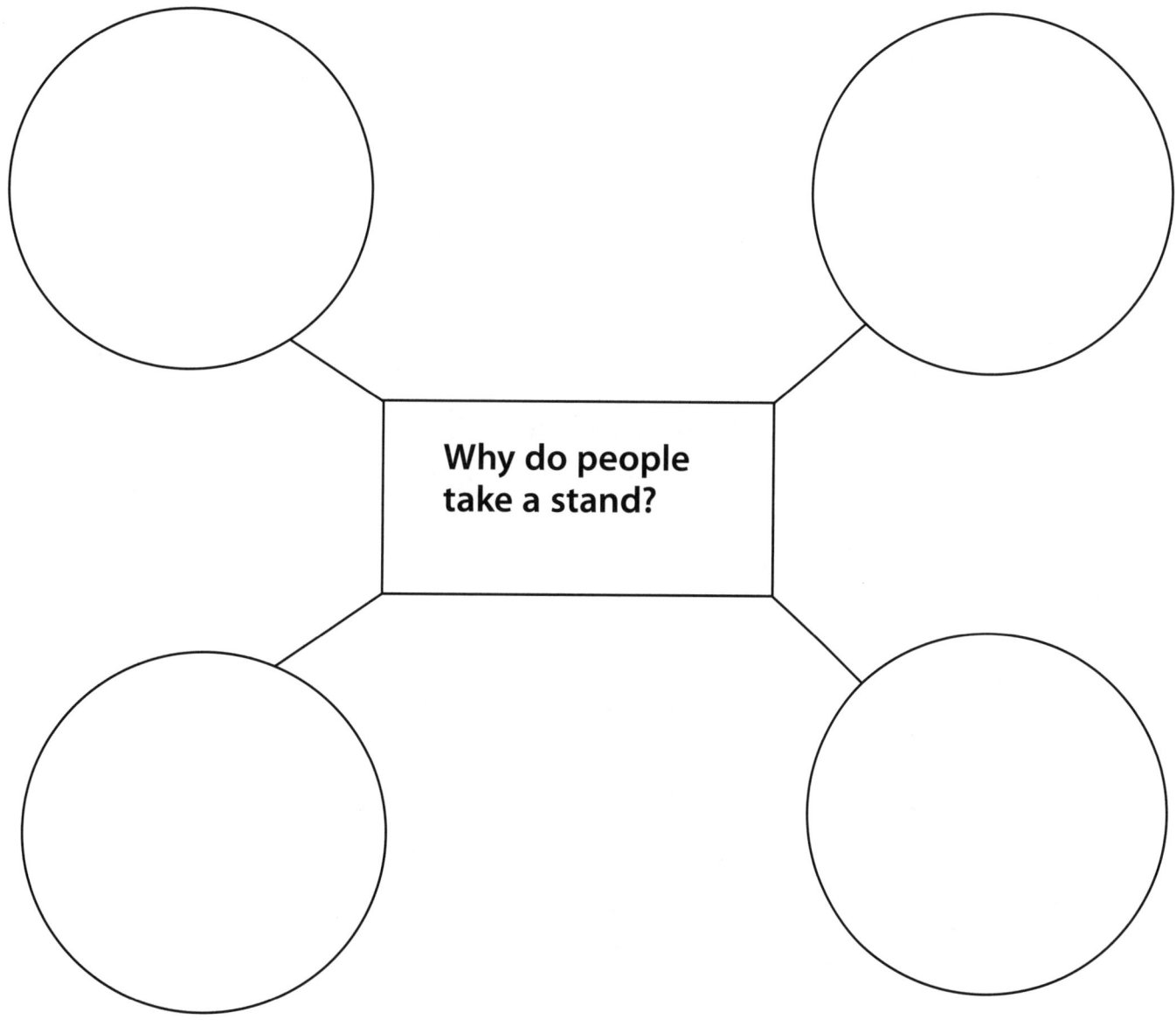

5.1   Unit 5 | A Time to Act

Name _____ Date _____

Thinking Map

Relate Ideas

Make a main idea web with a main idea and supporting details.

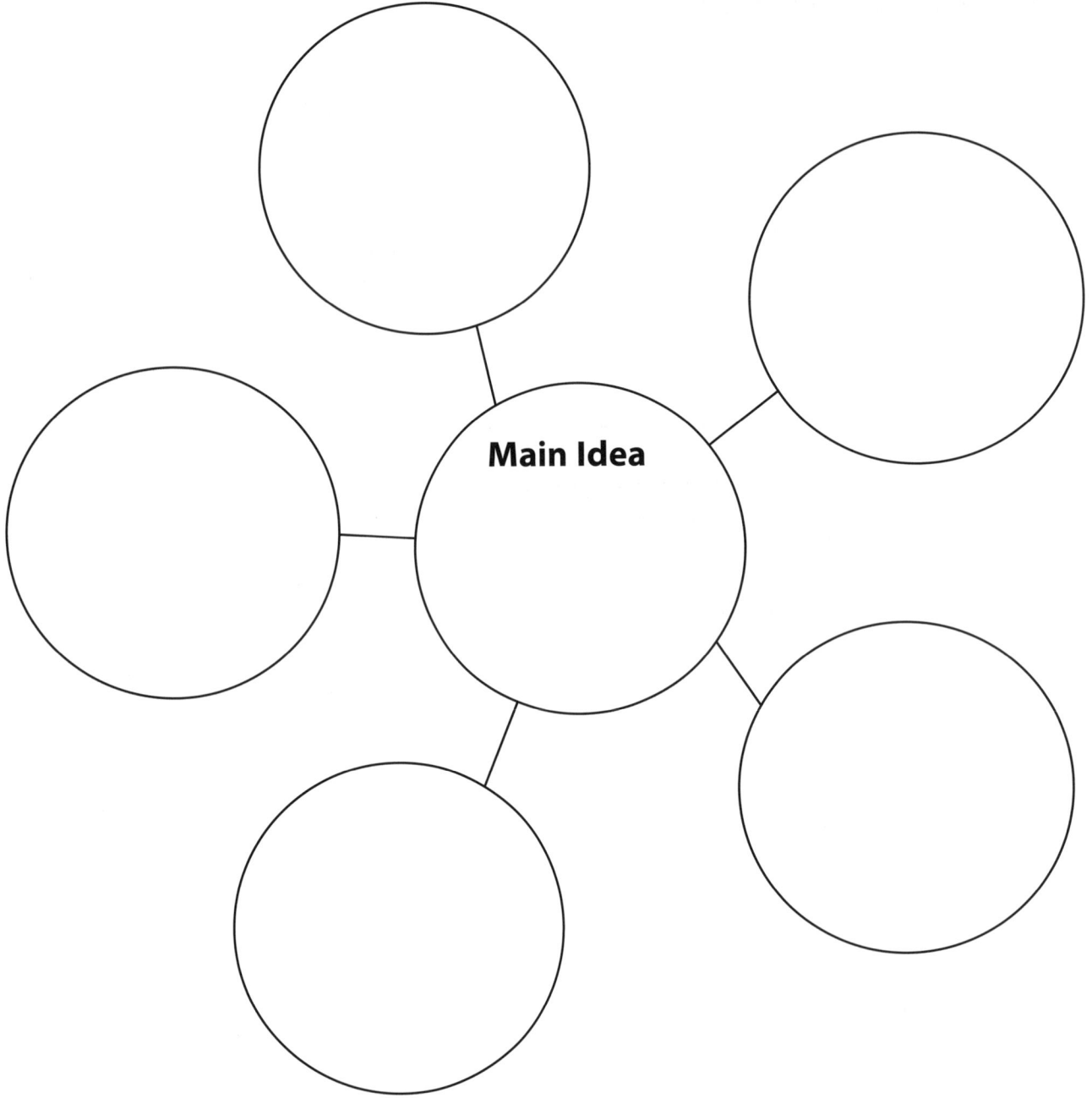

Use your main idea web to explain how the main idea and supporting details of the event are related.

5.2   Unit 5 | A Time to Act

Name _____ Date _____

Grammar

It Happened in the Past

1. Play with a partner.

2. Use a paper clip or other small object as a game marker. Place one marker on each START.

3. Flip a coin to move up the ladder. Heads = 1 step; tails = 2 steps.

4. Read the **verb** on the step where you land. Change it to form the **past tense**. Use the past tense verb in a sentence.

5. If your partner agrees that you formed and used the word correctly, stay on that step. If not, move back down one step.

6. Take turns. The first player to reach END is the winner.

END	END
cry	walk
protest	are
ride	has
change	stop
has	cry
walk	change
stop	protest
are	ride
START Player 1	**START** Player 2

5.3

Unit 5 | A Time to Act

Name _____   Date _____

Key Points Reading

"The Civil Rights Movement"

Listen as your teacher reads. Follow with your finger.

1. During the 1950s, African Americans often faced discrimination. In the South, segregation laws kept blacks separate from whites in most public places. Many people thought these conditions were unfair. So they started the Civil Rights Movement to fight for equal rights.

2. As a lawyer, Thurgood Marshall brought many cases before the Supreme Court. One case was *Brown v. Board of Education*. Marshall argued that black students did not receive equal schooling. The Court ruled that school segregation was unconstitutional. Schools were ordered to integrate.

3. Martin Luther King, Jr. was a powerful speaker who encouraged peaceful protests. In 1955, he called for a boycott of public buses. The protest was effective. The bus company lost money. The Supreme Court ruled against segregation on buses.

All of these efforts helped to gain equal rights for African Americans.

Name _____   Date _____

Grammar

Race to the Future

Directions:

1. Play with a partner.

2. Use a paper clip, eraser, or other small object as a game marker. Place it on START.

3. Flip a coin to move ahead. Heads = 1 space; tails = 2 spaces.

4. Read the **verb** on the space where you land. Write its **future tense** form and use it in a sentence.

5. If your partner agrees that you formed and used the future tense correctly, stay where you are. If not, go back one space.

6. Take turns. The first player to reach FINISH is the winner.

START	work	do	share	finish	join
					believe
fight	march	protest	boycott	occupy	divide
drive					
observe	arrest	stop	charge	deny	FINISH

5.5

Unit 5 | A Time to Act

Name _____   Date _____

Reread and Retell

"The Civil Rights Movement"

Make a main idea web with a main idea and supporting details.

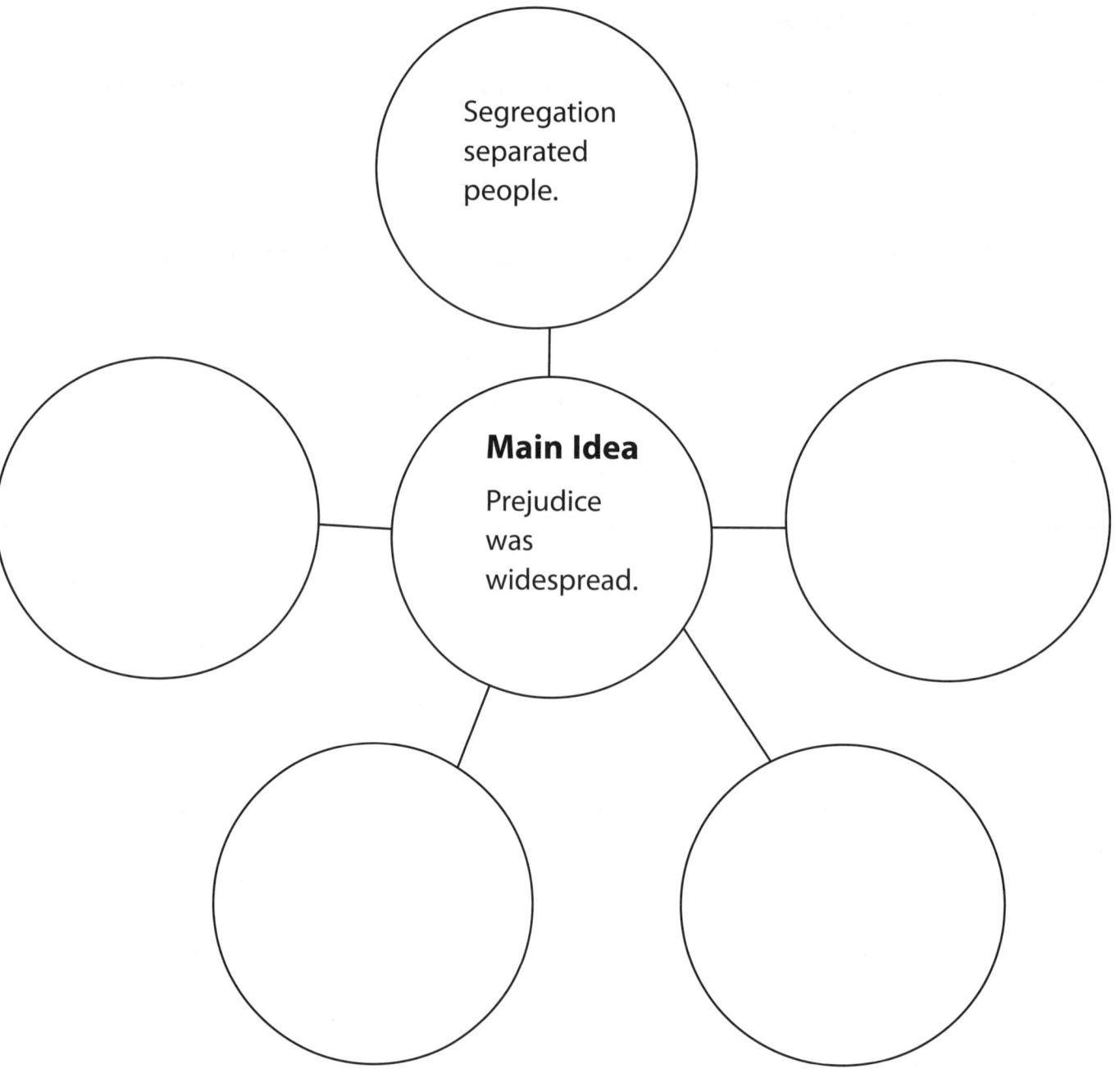

🗨 Use your main idea web to summarize "The Civil Rights Movement" to a partner.

5.6   Unit 5 | A Time to Act

Name _____   Date _____

Fluency

"The Civil Rights Movement"

Use this passage to practice reading with proper intonation.

In June 1963, President Kennedy demanded that Congress	8
pass a strong civil rights bill. In a speech to the nation he asked,	22
"Are we to say to the world—and much more importantly to each	35
other—that this is the land of the free, except for the Negroes?"	48
To persuade Congress to pass the bill, civil rights leaders	58
A. Philip Randolph and Bayard Rustin organized a huge march on	69
Washington, DC. On August 28, more than 250,000 people—both	79
African Americans and whites—came together in the nation's capital.	89
Labor unions and religious leaders joined the protest.	97
It was the largest show of support for the Civil Rights Movement	109
so far. The march ended at the Lincoln Memorial. For three hours, the	122
crowd listened to a lot of speeches.	129

From "The Civil Rights Movement," page 25

Intonation

1. ☐ Does not change pitch.
2. ☐ Changes pitch, but does not match content.
3. ☐ Changes pitch to match some of the content.
4. ☐ Changes pitch to match all of the content.

Accuracy and Rate Formula

Use the formula to measure a reader's accuracy and rate while reading aloud.

_____ − _____ = _____
words attempted   number of errors   words correct per minute
in one minute   (wcpm)

5.7   Unit 5 | A Time to Act

Name _____   Date _____

Reading Options

"Rosa Parks: My Story"

Complete the chart as you read the memoir.

Page	What I read	What it means to me

▶ Do you think you would have responded the same way as Rosa Parks did? Tell a partner why or why not.

Name _____ Date _____

Respond and Extend

Compare Accounts

Complete the Venn diagram to compare and contrast Kevin Supples's and Rosa Parks's accounts of Rosa Parks's experience.

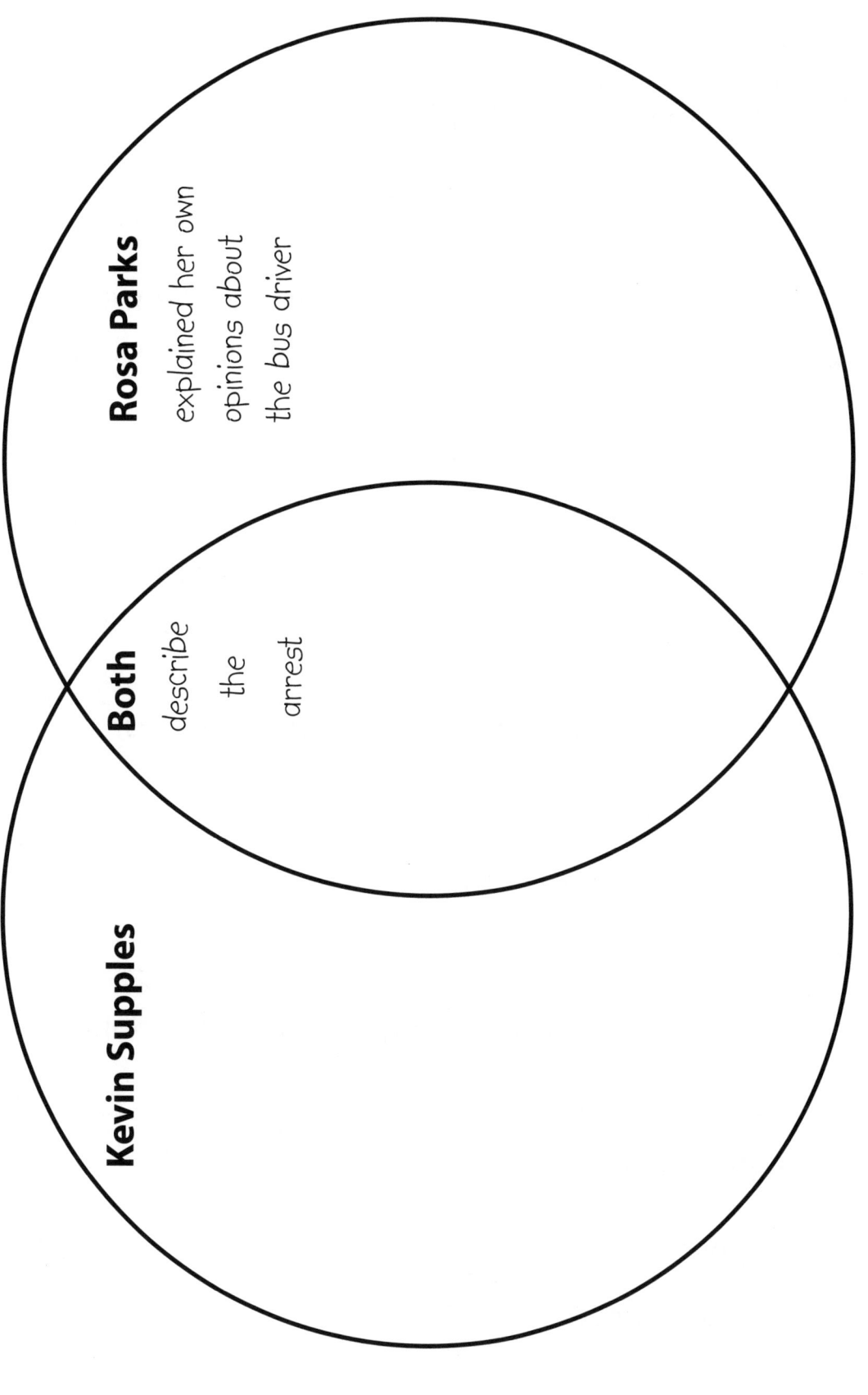

Rosa Parks: explained her own opinions about the bus driver

Both: describe the arrest

Kevin Supples

5.9 — Unit 5 | A Time to Act

Name _____ Date _____

Grammar

School Segregation

Grammar Rules Verb Tenses

1. For most verbs, add **-ed** to show past tense.
2. For some verbs, change the spelling of the base word before you add **-ed**.
3. Irregular verbs have special forms to show past tense.
4. Use **will** before the **main verb** to show future tense.
5. You can also use **am going to**, **are going to**, or **is going to** before the **main verb** to show future tense.

Write the form of the verb shown in parentheses.

1. In 1951, Thurgood Marshall _____ an important case to the Supreme Court.
   (past tense of *bring*)

2. In 1954, the Court _____ that segregation in public schools was unconstitutional.
   (past tense of *declare*)

3. The case _____ the rights of all students in the future.
   (future tense of *protect*)

4. People _____ Thurgood Marshall for a long time.
   (future tense of *remember*)

🗨 **Tell a partner about an important right that people gained in the past and one that people hope to gain in the future.**

5.10   Unit 5 | A Time to Act

Name _____ Date _____

Close Reading

from "Rosa Parks: My Story,"
pages 30–31

Analyze the text below with your teacher and make notes.

1   "Y'all better make it light on yourselves and let me have those seats."

2   The man in the window seat next to me stood up, and I moved to let him pass by me, and then I looked across the aisle and saw that the two women were also standing. I moved over to the window seat. I could not see how standing up was going to "make it light" for me. The more we gave in and complied, the worse they treated us.

3   I thought back to the time when I used to sit up all night and didn't sleep, and my grandfather would have his gun right by the fireplace, or if he had his one-horse wagon going anywhere, he always had his gun in the back of the wagon. People always say that I didn't give up my seat because I was tired, but that isn't true. I was not tired physically, or no more tired than I usually was at the end of a working day. I was not old, although some people have an image of me as being old then. I was forty-two. No, the only tired I was, was tired of giving in.

Close Reading

from "Rosa Parks: My Story," page 33

Make notes as you read the paragraphs below. Then answer the questions on page 5.13.

1. Meanwhile there were people getting off the bus and asking for transfers, so that began to loosen up the crowd, especially in the back of the bus. Not everyone got off, but everybody was very quiet. What conversation there was, was in low tones; no one was talking out loud. It would have been quite interesting to have seen the whole bus empty out. Or if the other three had stayed where they were, because if they'd had to arrest four of us instead of one, then that would have given me a little support. But it didn't matter. I never thought hard of them at all and never even bothered to criticize them.

2. Eventually two policemen came. They got on the bus, and one of them asked me why I didn't stand up. I asked him, "Why do you all push us around?" He said to me, and I quote him exactly, "I don't know, but the law is the law and you're under arrest."

Name _____   Date _____

Close Reading

from "Rosa Parks: My Story" (continued)

Reread and annotate the passage to answer these questions.

Reread paragraph 1.

1. What did the other passengers do while Rosa Parks stayed in her bus seat? Highlight text evidence that supports your answer.

2. Parks wished that either everyone would have gotten off the bus or that the other African American passengers in her row would have stayed and been arrested, too. Why? Highlight text evidence.

3. Parks writes that she "never thought hard" about the other passengers, which means that she was never angry at them. Highlight text evidence that supports Parks's claim. Why do you think Parks felt this way?

Reread paragraph 2.

4. Underline this sentence: "Why do you all push us around?" The phrase "push us around" means "cause problems for us" or "be mean to us." Who was Parks talking about when she said "you" and "us"?

Name _____ Date _____

Thinking Map

Theme

Identify a story's theme by using its details.

Details from the title:	Details from the characters:
Details from the setting:	**Details from the plot:**

Theme:

▬ Use your theme chart to explain to a partner how the details from the title, characters, setting, and plot help you identify the theme of the story.

5.14

Unit 5 | A Time to Act

Name _____ Date _____

Grammar

Present Perfect Tense: I Have Done That!

1. Play with a partner. Make word cards. Stack them face down. Put the white cards in one stack and the gray cards in another.

2. Take turns. Draw one card from each stack. Form a sentence in the **present perfect** tense, using the words on your cards.

3. If your partner agrees that your sentence is correct, you get one point. Then your partner takes a turn.

4. The first player to get five points wins. If both players get five points in the same turn, the game is a tie.

I	She	It
We	You	They
help	be	take
ride	protest	go
throw	speak	look
do	see	study

© Cengage Learning, Inc.

5.15

Unit 5 | A Time to Act

Name _____ Date _____

Key Points Reading

"Ayanna Sits In"

Listen as your teacher reads. Follow with your finger.

1. It's 1957. Ayanna and her classmates are from Oklahoma City. They visit New York City and are surprised to be served in a restaurant with white customers, because they are African American. The South, where they live, is still segregated. In their town, they aren't allowed to swim in public pools, stay in hotels, or live in white neighborhoods.

2. Ayanna and the rest of the Youth Council decide they need to make a change back home. They go to a drugstore lunch counter and ask for sodas. The manager tells them they can't stay. But they don't leave. They sit quietly and wait, and then they do it again the next day.

3. When they arrive on the third day, they get a surprise. They order their sodas, and the waitress serves them. They've won—the owners have decided to end segregation at their whole chain of drugstores. Ayanna and her friends continue to participate in other sit-ins until more laws change.

Name _____ Date _____

Grammar

Past and Future Perfect Tenses: Spin a Tense

1. Play with a partner. Take turns.
2. Spin the paper clip. Read the verb.
3. Write a sentence using the **past perfect** form of the verb.
4. If your partner agrees that you have used the tense correctly and that you have spelled the main verb correctly, score one point.
5. Then your partner takes a turn.
6. After all the verbs have been used once, repeat the game using the **future perfect** tense.
7. Count your points. The player with the most points wins.

Make a Spinner
1. Place one loop of a paper clip over the center of the circle.
2. Push a sharp pencil through the loop and the paper.
3. Spin the paper clip around the pencil.

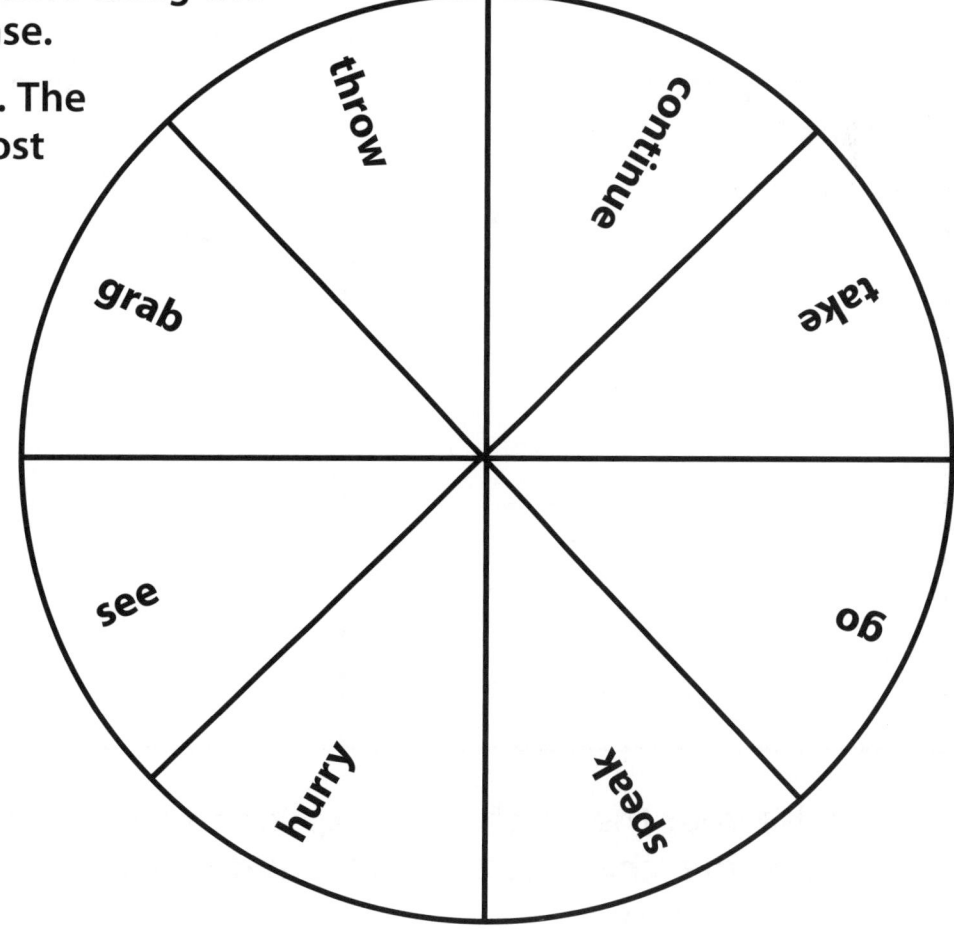

5.17 Unit 5 | A Time to Act

Name _____   Date _____

Reread and Retell

"Ayanna Sits In"

Identify the story's theme by using its details.

Details from the title:	Details from the characters:
	Ayanna is surprised that African Americans are treated equally in New York.
Details from the setting:	**Details from the plot:**

Theme:

 Use your theme chart to explain to a partner how the details from the title, characters, setting, and plot help you identify the theme of the story.

Name _____ Date _____

Fluency

"Ayanna Sits In"

Use this passage to practice reading with proper expression.

Mrs. Luper led the group down the street to a restaurant. She held	13
the door open.	16
The kids stopped. They looked at Mrs. Luper.	24
Calvin frowned. "Are we all going in?"	31
"We are," said Mrs. Luper.	36
"Are we getting food to take with us on the bus?" Ayanna whispered.	49
"We are not," said Mrs. Luper in a firm, unwavering voice.	60
Ayanna knew that voice. It was the voice Mrs. Luper used when she	73
was determined to do the right thing and not let anyone stop her—and	87
make sure the kids did the right thing, too.	96
Mrs. Luper used that voice a lot.	103

From "Ayanna Sits In," pages 47–48

Expression

1. ☐ Does not read with feeling.
2. ☐ Reads with some feeling, but does not match content.
3. ☐ Reads with appropriate feeling for most content.
4. ☐ Reads with appropriate feeling for all content.

Accuracy and Rate Formula

Use the formula to measure a reader's accuracy and rate while reading aloud.

_____ − _____ = _____
words attempted in one minute   number of errors   words correct per minute (wcpm)

5.19   Unit 5 | A Time to Act

Name _____   Date _____

Reading Options

"Roll of Thunder, Hear My Cry"

Complete the chart as you read the story.

Page	What I read	What it reminds me of

💬 Tell a partner which detail was most interesting and why.

Name _____ Date _____

Respond and Extend

Compare Themes

Use a comparison chart to compare two stories.

Themes	"Ayanna Sits In"	"Roll of Thunder, Hear My Cry"
People should stand up to injustices.	Ayanna agrees to participate in the sit-in at the restaurant.	
Taking a stand can cause problems.		

Talk with a partner about the themes in each selection. How did the characters from each story take a stand?

© Cengage Learning, Inc.

Name _____ Date _____

Grammar

Cassie and the New Books

Grammar Rules: Perfect Tense Verbs

1. Use the **present perfect** tense for actions that began in the past and are still going on.
2. Use the **past perfect** tense for actions completed before another past action.
3. Use the **future perfect** tense for actions that will happen before a future time.

Rewrite each sentence so the underlined verb is in the perfect tense given in parentheses.

1. Miss Crocker moves Cassie's seat. (past perfect)

   _____

2. The superintendent takes the books to school. (present perfect)

   _____

3. Cassie starts reading during Miss Crocker's talk. (past perfect)

   _____

4. Before school ends, Miss Crocker punishes Cassie. (future perfect)

   _____

5. By dinnertime, Cassie talks to Mama. (future perfect)

   _____

🗨 Say a sentence with a present perfect, past perfect, or future perfect verb. Ask a partner to identify the verb tense. Then switch roles.

Name _____ Date _____

Close Reading

from "Roll of Thunder, Hear My Cry," page 68

Analyze the text below with your teacher and make notes.

1   [Little Man's] lips parted slightly as he took his hands from the book. He quivered, but he did not take his eyes from Miss Crocker. "I—I said may I have another book please, ma'am," he squeaked. "That one's dirty."

2   "Dirty!" Miss Crocker echoed, appalled by such temerity. She stood up, gazing down upon Little Man like a bony giant, but Little Man raised his head and continued to look into her eyes. "Dirty! And just who do you think you are, Clayton Chester? Here the county is giving us these wonderful books during these hard times and you're going to stand there and tell me that the book's too dirty? Now you take that book or get nothing at all!"

Close Reading

from "Roll of Thunder, Hear My Cry," page 71

Make notes as you read the paragraphs below. Then answer the questions on page 5.25.

1. "See, Miz Crocker, see what it says. They give us these ole books when they didn't want 'em no more."

2. She regarded me impatiently, but did not look at the book. "Now how could he know what it says? He can't read."

3. "Yes'm, he can. He been reading since he was four. He can't read all them big words, but he can read them columns. See what's in the last row. Please look, Miz Crocker."

4. This time Miss Crocker did look, but her face did not change. Then, holding up her head, she gazed unblinkingly down at me.

5. "S-see what they called us," I said, afraid she had not seen.

6. "That's what you are," she said coldly. "Now go sit down."

7. I shook my head, realizing now that Miss Crocker did not even know what I was talking about. She had looked at the page and had understood nothing.

8. "I said sit down, Cassie!"

9. I started slowly toward my desk, but as the hickory stick sliced the tense air, I turned back around. "Miz Crocker," I said, "I don't want my book neither."

Name _____ Date _____

Close Reading

from "Roll of Thunder, Hear My Cry" (continued)

Reread and annotate the passage to answer these questions.

Reread paragraphs 1–3.

1. What are two reasons Little Man and Cassie don't want the books? Highlight text evidence that supports your answer.

Reread paragraphs 4–6.

2. Miss Crocker looks at the last column of the chart and sees what is written there. Use text evidence to summarize Miss Crocker's reaction. What does this tell you about her?

Reread paragraphs 7–9.

3. Cassie feels that Miss Crocker "did not even know what I was talking about" and "had understood nothing." What does Cassie mean?

4. What happens at the end of the passage? Summarize how Cassie's actions reflect the theme of taking a stand. Highlight text evidence.

Name _____ Date _____

Writing Project

Ideas

Writing is well-developed when the message is clear and interesting to the reader. It is supported by details that show the writer knows the topic well.

	Is the argument clear and focused?	**Do the details show that the writer knows the topic?**
4 Wow!	❑ The argument has a clear and focused claim and includes signal words to link the claim to the reasons. ❑ The writing keeps me interested.	❑ All the facts and details are accurate and relevant to the claim. ❑ The writer knows the topic well.
3 Ahh.	❑ The argument has a fairly clear and focused claim and includes some signal words to link the claim to the reasons. ❑ Most of the writing keeps me interested.	❑ Most of the facts and details are accurate and relevant to the claim. ❑ The writer knows the topic fairly well.
2 Hmm.	❑ The claim is somewhat unclear and unfocused. It feels a little unconnected to the reasons. ❑ Some of the writing keeps me interested.	❑ Some of the facts and details are not accurate or relevant to the claim. ❑ The writer does not know the topic very well.
1 Huh?	❑ The claim is unclear and unfocused. It does not feel connected to the reasons. ❑ The writing is too confusing to keep my interest.	❑ Many of the facts and details are not accurate or relevant to the claim. ❑ The writer does not know the topic well at all.

Name _____   Date _____

Writing Project

Claim-and-Evidence Chart

Complete the chart for your persuasive speech.

Claim	Reasons and evidence	Action needed
	Reason 1: Evidence: Reason 2: Evidence:	

5.27 | Unit 5 | A Time to Act

Name _____ Date _____

Writing Project

Revise

Use revision marks to make changes to these paragraphs. Look for:

- an introduction that grabs the reader's attention
- signal words that connect ideas
- strong, formal language that appeals to emotions

Revision Marks	
∧	Add
℘	Take out
⌒⌒	Move to here
∧̓	Insert comma
/	Make lowercase

Stop Cyberbullying Now!

If you or someone you know has been bullied online, then you know it is a problem. It is called cyberbullying, and it should be stopped.

Cyberbullying is dangerous. It makes the victim feel bad and can lead to depression. More than 50 percent of young people are affected by cyberbullying. It is important to stop it now before the numbers get larger.

Name _____ Date _____

Writing Project

Edit and Proofread

Use revision marks to edit and proofread these paragraphs. Look for:

- correct use of past tense, future tense, and perfect tense verbs
- correct spelling of irregular past tense verbs

Revision Marks	
∧	Add
℘	Take out

Stop Cyberbullying Now! (continued)

Before you has typed a mean message to someone, please stop and think. One report sayed that over 52 percent of cyberbullies never stopped and thinked about the effects of their hurtful words. If they had consider the victim's feelings first, they would not have posted the mean message.

Another way to stop cyberbullying is to ask for help. Kids should report any cyberbullying to a parent, teacher, or counselor. These adults will knew what to do. They will have punish the cyberbullies.

Cyberbullies has caused harm for years. Learn how to stop them before it is too late!

Name _____   Date _____

Unit Concept Map

Food for Thought

Make a concept map with the answers to the Big Question:
How can we feed a growing planet?

Problem
How can we feed a growing planet?

On a Local Level
- start a community garden
-
-
-
-

On a National or Global Level
-
-
-
-

Solution

6.1

Unit 6 | Food for Thought

© Cengage Learning, Inc.

Name _____   Date _____

Thinking Map

Plot and Character

Make a double sequence chain about events and responses.

Events

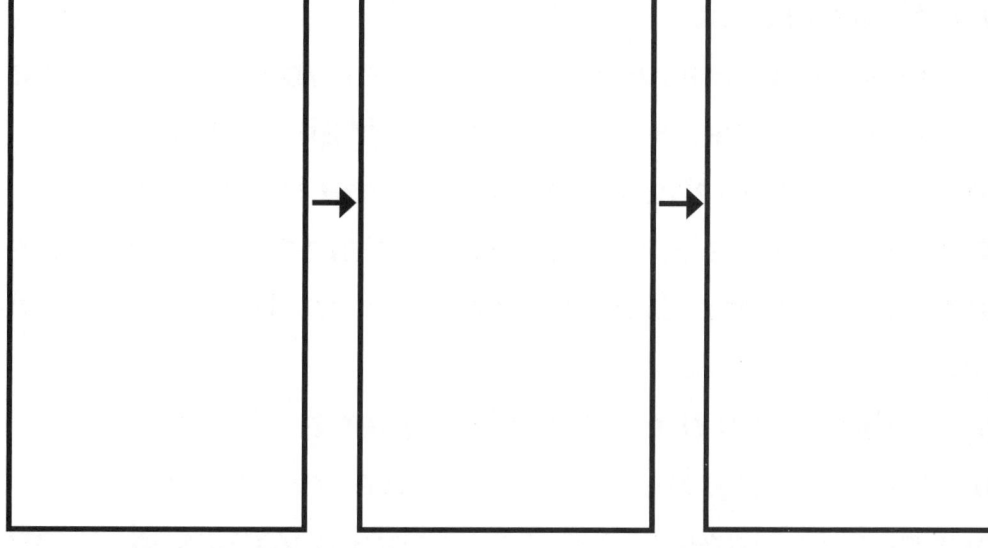

Character's Response

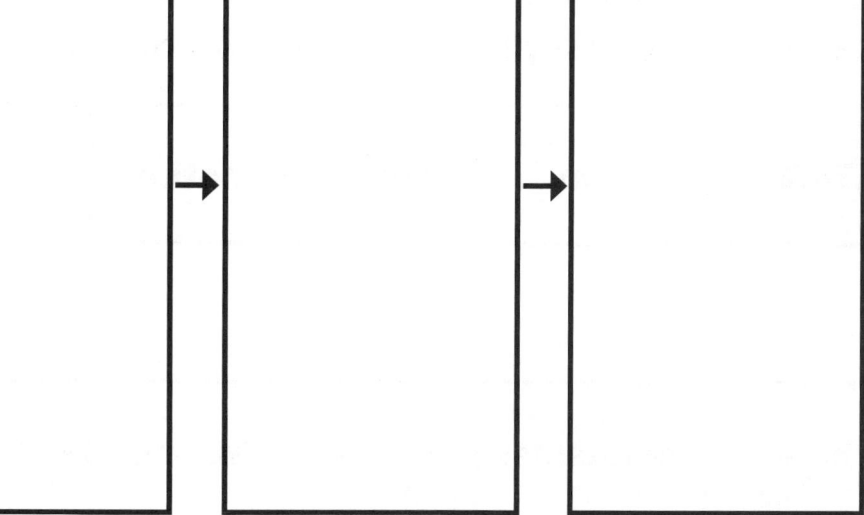

 Tell a partner a story from your life and how you responded to the events. Have your partner use the double sequence chain to record the events and your responses.

6.2

Unit 6 | Food for Thought

Grammar

Pronouns: Agree with the Antecedent

1. Play with a partner.
2. Use a paper clip, eraser, or other small object as a game piece.
3. Flip a coin to move. Heads = 1 space; tails = 2 spaces.
4. Read the **noun** on the space where you land. Say it in a sentence. Then make up a second related sentence. Use a **pronoun** that refers back to the noun in the first sentence. For example:

    <u>Kim</u> walks down the street. <u>She</u> goes to the lot.

    Virgil dug a <u>hole</u>. He put the lettuce seeds in <u>it</u>.
5. If your partner agrees that the pronoun you used is correct, stay where you are. If not, go back one space.
6. Take turns. The first player to reach FINISH wins.

START	Kim	father	mother	beans	plan
					garden
bike	vegetables	shovel	Marcus	Miss Fleck	seeds
neighbors					
city	women	friends	class	children	FINISH

Name _____ Date _____

Key Points Reading

"Seedfolks"

Listen as your teacher reads. Follow with your finger.

1

A group of neighbors in Cleveland, Ohio, share a community garden. Three people tell about their experiences in the garden. Kim is a young girl whose father had been a farmer in Vietnam. However, Kim never met her father because he died before she was born. She plants bean seeds to feel connected to him.

2

Virgil and his father plant several plots of baby lettuce. His father envisions selling the lettuce to fancy restaurants. If they make enough money, Virgil will get a new bike. Virgil devotes his time to tending to the lettuce, but it wilts and shrivels up. Virgil feels bad for his father. He hopes the lettuce can be saved.

3

Amir is an Indian immigrant who plants several types of vegetables. Before taking part in the garden, he didn't know many of his neighbors. But now, he and his neighbors grow closer as a community. They work together and get to know one another better as they talk about their gardens.

Name _____ Date _____

Grammar

Pronoun Tic-Tac-Toe

1. Play with a partner. Take turns.
2. Choose two squares. Read the words on them. Use the words to form a **compound subject or object**, and say it in a sentence. Then say the sentence again, but replace the compound subject or object with the correct **pronoun**. Example: <u>Virgil</u> and <u>I</u> went to the park. <u>We</u> went to the park.
3. If your partner agrees that your second sentence is correct, write your initials in both squares.
4. The first player to get five squares in a row across or down is the winner. If neither player has five in a row, the player with the most squares wins.

Virgil	me	garden	neighbor	eggplant
seeds	father	lettuce	grandmother	me
I	shovel	**FREE**	spoon	sister
woman	Amir	table	I	hat
people	Miss Fleck	chair	locket	uncle

6.5

Unit 6 | Food for Thought

Name _____ Date _____

Vocabulary

Vocabulary Bingo

Play Bingo using the Key Words from this unit.

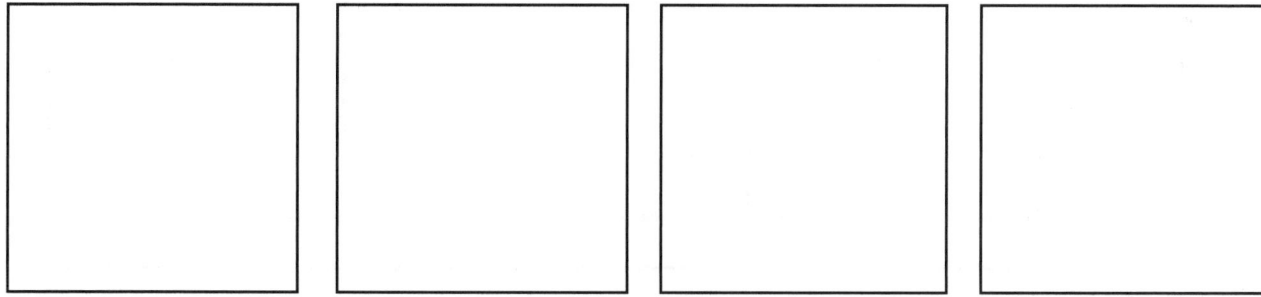
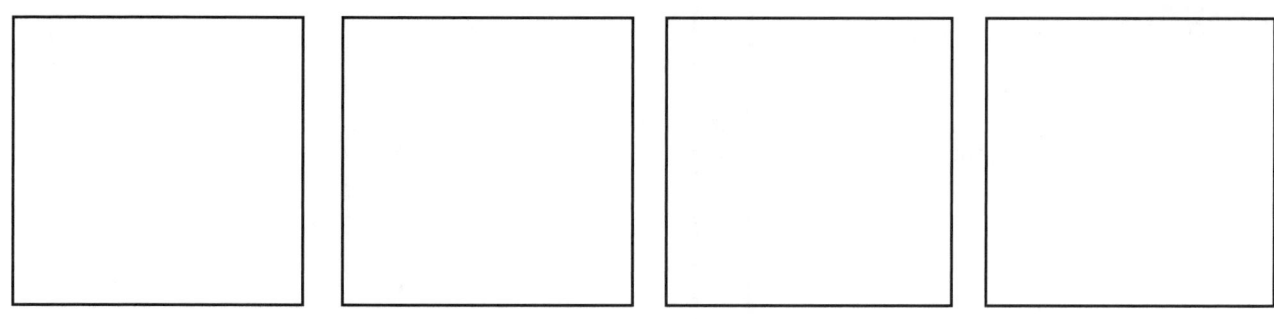

6.6 Unit 6 | Food for Thought

Name _____   Date _____

Reread and Retell

"Seedfolks"

Make a double sequence chain for "Seedfolks."

Story Events

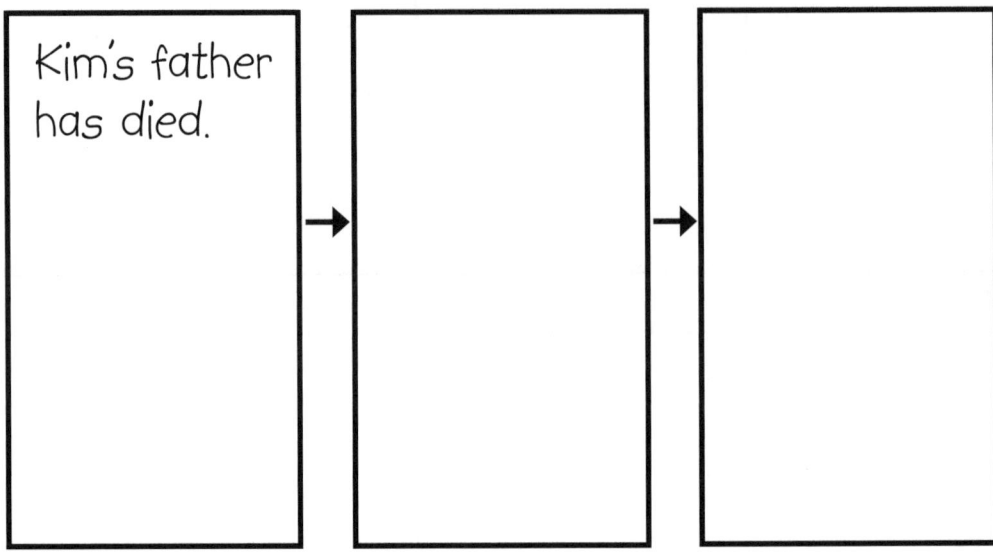

Character's Response

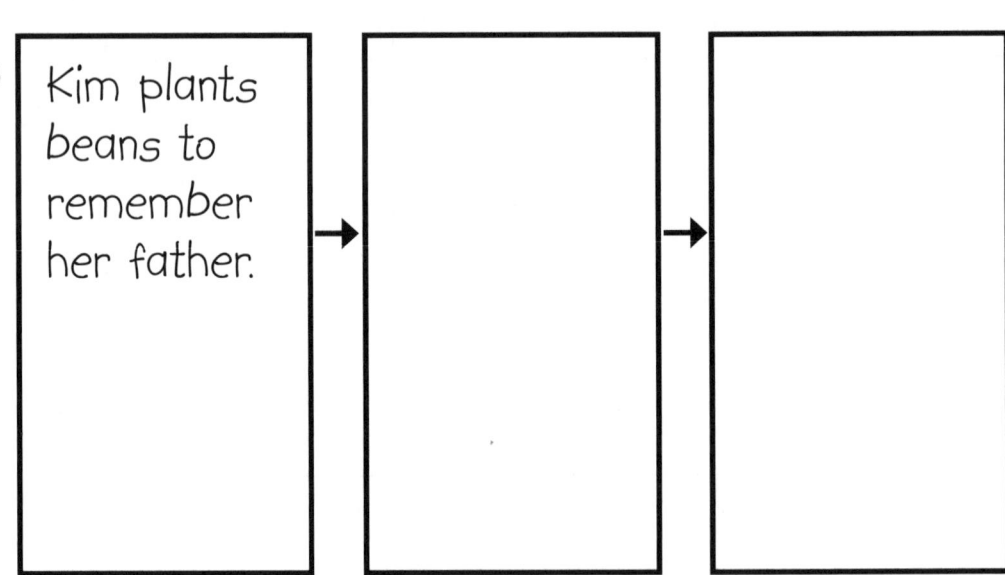

Work with a partner to complete a double sequence chain that summarizes the events and the characters' responses to the events. Then use the completed double sequence chain to retell the story.

Name _____ Date _____

Fluency

"Seedfolks"

Use this passage to practice reading with proper intonation.

I couldn't believe it. I stomped outside. I could feel that	11
eighteen-speed slipping away. I was used to seeing kids lying	22
and making mistakes, but not grown-ups. I was mad at my	34
father. Then I sort of felt sorry for him.	43
That night I pulled out the locket. I opened it up and looked	56
at the picture. We'd studied Greek myths in school that year.	67
In our book, the goddess of crops and the earth had a sad mouth	81
and flowers around her, just like the girl in the locket. I scraped	94
off the rust with our dish scrubber and shined up that locket as	107
bright as I could get it. Then I opened it up, just a crack. Then	122
I whispered, "Save our lettuce," to the girl.	130

From "Seedfolks," page 100

Intonation

- [1] ☐ Does not change pitch.
- [2] ☐ Changes pitch but does not match content.
- [3] ☐ Changes pitch to match some of the content.
- [4] ☐ Changes pitch to match all of the content.

Accuracy and Rate Formula
Use the formula to measure a reader's accuracy and rate while reading aloud.

_____ − _____ = _____
words attempted   number of errors   words correct per minute
in one minute   (wcpm)

Name _____ Date _____

Reading Options

"Soul-Soothing Soups"

Complete the chart as you read the interview.

What I think	What my partner thinks
Page _____	_____
Page _____	_____
Page _____	_____
Page _____	_____

 Tell a partner your thoughts about each page. Then ask your partner to share his or her thoughts.

Name _____ Date _____

Respond and Extend

Compare Viewpoints

Use a comparison chart to compare viewpoints from the two texts.

"Seedfolks" Kim	"Seedfolks" Virgil	"Seedfolks" Amir	"Soul-Soothing Soups" Mary Ellen Diaz
Viewpoint: feels the garden will bring her closer to her dead father and help her father get to know her	**Viewpoint:**	**Viewpoint:**	**Viewpoint:**
Details: • •	**Details:** • •	**Details:** • •	**Details:** • •

▸ Use your chart to record viewpoints about the benefits of gardens and nutritious meals. Work with a partner to find evidence and details that support the viewpoints.

Name _____ Date _____

Grammar

Virgil's Garden

Grammar Rules Correct Pronouns

1. A **pronoun** must agree with its **antecedent** in number and person.
2. Use a **singular pronoun** for one person or thing.
3. Use a **plural pronoun** for more than one person or thing.
4. Use **I** and **me** to refer to yourself. Use **we** and **us** to refer to yourself and one or more other people.
5. Use **you** to address one or more persons.
6. Use **he** and **him** to refer to males. Use **she** and **her** to refer to females. Use **it** to refer to a thing.
7. Use **they** and **them** to refer to more than one person or thing.

Read the sentences. Write the correct pronoun in the blank. Then underline the antecedent.

1. Virgil had a garden. _____ grew lettuce.

2. Auntie had a garden plot. Virgil took care of the plot for _____.

3. The leaves shriveled up. Then _____ turned yellow.

4. Virgil wanted a bike. _____ had 18 speeds.

5. Virgil said, "_____ worry about the lettuce plants."

 Use three sentences with pronouns to tell about the ways that we can help feed a growing planet. Ask a partner to identify the pronouns and their antecedents in your sentences.

Close Reading

from "Soul-Soothing Soups," page 111

Analyze the text below with your teacher and make notes.

1 **Q: What inspired you to leave your job as a chef and launch First Slice?**

2 **A:** I had a great restaurant career, but I felt like I had to make a choice about whether or not to stay. I wanted to be home at night reading books to my little girl instead of slaving away in the kitchen. I was also reading a lot about Jane Addams. She ran her own community kitchen that served food to people living on the street. She also helped women who were trying to enter the workforce. Jane Addams is still very much the inspiration for First Slice. I also started volunteering in the soup kitchens, and I realized feeding forty to fifty people takes talent. I never thought of using my skills that way until then.

3 **Q: What kind of food do you cook at First Slice?**

4 **A:** We made a lot of Cajun food to feed displaced victims of Hurricane Katrina. We also get a lot of requests for food with Latin flavors, dishes that might use tortillas. Smothered pork chops are really popular. A pot of greens is definitely a big thing, because most people on the street don't have access to farm-fresh produce.

Name _____ Date _____

Close Reading

from "Soul-Soothing Soups," pages 112–113

Make notes as you read the paragraphs below. Then answer the questions on page 6.14.

1 **Q: How do you work with volunteers?**

2 **A:** There's a food writer who comes in four hours a week and all she does is roll pie dough for us. She just loves pie dough. We serve a lot of pie, and making pie dough is really therapeutic. There's a man who comes in and just wants to chop onions. He recently applied for a job at a new gourmet store. He didn't get it, but I was thrilled that chopping onions gave him the confidence to start looking for a job; he's been out of work for so many years.

3 **Q: What's the best way for people to help feed the homeless?**

4 **A:** Make a connection with a food pantry and find a way to donate nutritious food. Fresh fruit and vegetables are always appreciated. Canned beans are always great to have around. Rice, dried grains, canned tomatoes, and jarred salsa are also good to have.

Name _____ Date _____

Close Reading

from "Soul-Soothing Soups" (continued)

Reread and annotate the passage to answer these questions.

Reread paragraphs 1–2.

1. *Therapeutic* means "good for you" or "healing." Make inferences about the food writer's volunteerism. How does her volunteerism help both the food writer and the homeless people who come to First Slice?

2. How did chopping onions help the man who volunteers at First Slice? Highlight text evidence that supports your answer.

Reread paragraphs 3–4.

3. Diaz says one of the best ways to help feed the homeless is to "make a connection with a food pantry." Make an inference about what Diaz means. Why would "making a connection" be so helpful?

4. What kinds of foods does Diaz recommend for people to donate? Highlight text evidence.

Name _____ Date _____

Thinking Map

Argument

Use the chart to write about what students can do to reduce global hunger.

Argument/Claim	Support	Type of evidence

 With a partner, discuss what students can do to help reduce global hunger. Record your partner's argument and support. Discuss whether the claim is based on facts or opinions and record your answer.

6.15   Unit 6 | Food for Thought

Name _____ Date _____

Grammar

Choose the Correct Pronoun

Read each sentence. Choose the pronoun that best matches the verb and the meaning of the sentence. Write the pronoun.

1. That lot is full of weeds and trash. _____ has cleaned it up for a long time. (Nobody/Somebody)

2. _____ is making a noise. Is it the farmer's truck? (Nothing/Something)

3. The restaurant is crowded every night. _____ go there for the big salads. (Many/Few)

4. The whole village harvests the crop. _____ helps. (Everyone/Several)

5. I buy all my fruit at that store because _____ tastes fresh. (everything/something)

6. Five students worked in the school garden. _____ planted a different type of seed. (Anyone/Each)

7. _____ is an interesting book. (This/These)

8. _____ is a huge building over there. (That/Those)

9. Do you see _____ in my hand? They are genetically modified beans. (this/these)

10. _____ are locally-grown vegetables. (That/Those)

Key Points Reading

"The End of Plenty"

Listen as your teacher reads. Follow with your finger.

1

In recent years, more and more food has been produced by farmers around the world. However, prices have not decreased—instead, they have gone up, making it difficult for some people to have enough food. Population growth and changes in how people eat are causing a need for more food.

2

From the 1950s to 1990s, scientists introduced new growing methods that helped the world have a "green revolution," when the production of corn, rice, and wheat more than doubled. Some experts say we need something like this again.

3

The way we eat today is not as efficient as it used to be, and one reason is that people around the world now eat a lot more meat. Farmers need to grow more grain to feed the animals for meat than they would if we simply ate the grain itself.

Key Points Reading

"The End of Plenty" (continued)

④

⑤

The green-revolution solution in the past had focused on such methods as genetically modifying seeds and using harmful chemical fertilizers to increase crops. Agroecologists say that to solve the food crisis today, there are different methods that we need to follow. We must consider environmental and social impacts of food production for the long term.

New agroecology projects focus on sustainable and ecologically friendly practices. One method is to teach farmers to grow crops that produce healthy grains while also enriching the soil for future crops naturally. The long-term goal is to find a way for population and resources to grow in a balanced way.

Name _____ Date _____

Grammar

Pronoun Challenge

1. Play with a partner. Make word cards. Place the cards face down in two piles. Put verbs in one pile and pronouns in the other.
2. Take turns. Turn over the top card from each pile.
3. Use the verb and pronoun together in a sentence. Use the pronoun as a **reflexive pronoun**.
   Example: *The cat <u>amused</u> <u>itself</u> with an empty box.*
4. If your partner agrees that your sentence is correct, keep the cards. If not, put the cards back.
5. Play until all the cards have been used. The player with the most cards wins.
6. Play again. This time use just the pronoun cards. Use them as **intensive pronouns** in sentences.

amuse	wash	devote	introduce
teach	feed	help	dress
itself	ourselves	yourself	myself
himself	yourselves	herself	themselves

Name _____ Date _____

Reread and Retell

"The End of Plenty"

Identify arguments and claims in the persuasive article, and then record the support and evidence the author includes for each one.

Argument/Claim	Support	Type of evidence
The skyrocketing cost of food in 2008 was a wake-up call for the planet.	Increasing prices of corn, wheat, and rice caused riots and poverty.	Fact

Use the chart to summarize the article for a partner.

6.20   Unit 6 | Food for Thought

Name _____ Date _____

Fluency

"The End of Plenty"

Use this passage to practice reading with proper phrasing.

The skyrocketing cost of food in 2008 was a wake-up call for the planet.	14
Between 2005 and the summer of 2008, the price of wheat and corn tripled,	28
and the price of rice increased five times, causing food riots in nearly two	42
dozen countries and pushing 75 million more people into poverty. But unlike	54
previous occasions, this price increase came in a year when the world's	66
farmers had produced more grains than ever before. Simply put: for years,	78
the world has been consuming more food than it has been producing.	90
Joachim von Braun, then-Director General of the International Food Policy	100
Research Institute in Washington, DC, explained at the height of the crisis,	112
"Agricultural productivity growth is only 1 to 2 percent a year. This is too	126
low to meet population growth and increased demand."	134

From "The End of Plenty," page 125

Phrasing

1. ☐ Rarely pauses while reading the text.
2. ☐ Occasionally pauses while reading the text.
3. ☐ Frequently pauses at appropriate points in the text.
4. ☐ Consistently pauses at all appropriate points in the text.

Accuracy and Rate Formula
Use the formula to measure a reader's accuracy and rate while reading aloud.

_____   −   _____   =   _____
words attempted   number of errors   words correct per minute
in one minute   (wcpm)

Name _____ Date _____

Reading Options

"How Altered?"

List three interesting facts you read about in the persuasive article.

That's a fact!

An interesting fact about _____

is _____

_____

That's a fact!

An interesting fact about _____

is _____

_____

That's a fact!

One more interesting fact about _____

is _____

_____

🗨️ Tell a partner which fact was most interesting and why.

Name _____   Date _____

Respond and Extend

Compare Arguments

Use a comparison chart to compare the arguments and evidence in the two articles.

	Argument	Evidence, reasons, or facts
"The End of Plenty"	1.	• •
	2.	• •
"How Altered?"	1. GM foods can help with problems of food shortage and hunger.	• Genetic modifications increase crop yields. •
	2.	• •

Discuss the benefits and risks of various farming methods with a partner. Then record your findings in the chart. Use your chart to compare the authors' arguments.

6.23

Unit 6 | Food for Thought

Name _____   Date _____

Grammar

Altered Food

Grammar Rules Different Kinds of Pronouns

1. Use an **indefinite pronoun** such as **everyone**, **something**, **nobody**, **all**, or **many** when you're not naming a specific person or thing.
2. Use a **demonstrative pronoun** (**this**, **that**, **these**, or **those**) to point to a specific thing without naming it.
3. Use a **reflexive pronoun** when the object refers back to the subject. Reflexive pronouns end with **-self** or **-selves**.
4. Use an **intensive pronoun** to emphasize a noun or pronoun in a sentence. Intensive pronouns have the same form as reflexive pronouns.

Circle the pronoun that best completes each sentence. Write the pronoun on the line.

1. _____ must be done about world hunger.

    Nobody   Everyone   Something   Many

2. Many scientists _____ believe that genetic engineering of food can be helpful.

    herself   themselves   itself   yourselves

3. Foods containing genetically engineered ingredients are in our stores. _____ include pizza, ice cream, and cookies.

    These   That   This   Those

4. I ask _____ how these foods make me feel.

    himself   herself   ourselves   myself

🗨 Talk about genetically modified foods. Use different pronouns.

Name _____ Date _____

Close Reading

from "How Altered?" page 142

Analyze the text below with your teacher and make notes.

1 **IN FAVOR OF GENETICALLY MODIFIED FOODS**
New technology can help protect against hunger.

2   I was one in a family of nine children growing up on a small farm in Kenya's highlands. I learned firsthand about the enormous challenge of breaking the cycle of poverty and hunger in rural Africa. In fact, the reason I became a plant scientist was to help farmers like my mother. My mother sold the only cow our family owned to pay for my secondary education. This was a sacrifice because I, like most children in Kenya, was needed on the farm.

3   I have since made it my mission to alert others to the urgent need for new technology in Africa. New technology can help protect against hunger, environmental damage, and poverty. African growers desperately need access to the best management practices and fertilizer. They need better seeds and biotechnology to help improve crop production. Crop production is currently the lowest in the world per unit area of land. Traditional agricultural practices continue to produce only low yields and poor people.

Name _____ Date _____

Close Reading

from "How Altered?" page 143

Make notes as you read the paragraphs below. Then answer the questions on page 6.27.

1. **AGAINST GENETICALLY MODIFIED FOODS**
Genetically modified food is a risky form of technology.

2. Genetically modified (GM) food is not the best way to feed the world. In my opinion, GM food is a harmful and risky form of technology.

3. I do not think we should genetically modify our food because it harms plant and animal life. GM plants can accidentally mix with wild plants. When this happens, superweeds, or giant weeds, may grow. Farmers need to use stronger forms of pesticide to kill superweeds. Stronger pesticides are bad for other plants and for the air we breathe.

4. Animals are also affected by GM foods. Some GM corn crops are a major health risk to animals that eat them. A study done in the U.S. showed that 44 percent of caterpillars of the monarch butterfly died when fed large amounts of pollen, or powder, from GM corn.

5. We know that GM foods negatively affect plant and animal life. It is important to think about the risks GM foods pose to humans as well. Many experts caution against GM foods. Ronnie Cummins of the Organic Consumers Association warns, "We are rushing headlong into a new technology. We are courting disaster if we don't look before we leap."

Name _____ Date _____

Close Reading

from "How Altered?" (continued)

Reread and annotate the passage to answer these questions.

Reread paragraphs 1–2.

1. What is the writer's claim for his argument? Highlight text evidence to support your answer.

Reread paragraphs 3–4.

2. What is the main idea of paragraphs 3–4? List two details that support the main idea. Highlight text evidence.

Reread paragraph 5.

3. "Courting disaster" means "something horrible is going to happen." Why does Ronnie Cummins feel "we are courting disaster" if we don't spend more time studying GM foods? Highlight text evidence that supports your answer.

4. What makes this writer a trustworthy source for the argument against genetically modified foods?

6.27   Unit 6 | Food for Thought

Name _____   Date _____

Writing Project

Voice

Every writer has a special way of saying things, or a voice. The voice should sound genuine, or real, and be unique to that writer.

	Does the writing sound real and unique?	**Does the style fit the purpose and audience of an editorial?**
4 Wow!	❑ The writing sounds real and unique. It shows who the writer is. ❑ The writer uses different lengths and types of sentences to make the writing interesting.	❑ The tone is formal. ❑ The writer uses language that is strong and persuasive.
3 Ahh.	❑ Most of the writing sounds real and unique. ❑ The writer varies the sentences to make the writing fairly interesting.	❑ The tone is formal in most places. ❑ The language is mostly strong and persuasive.
2 Hmm.	❑ Only a few parts of the writing seem real and unique. ❑ The writer does not vary the lengths and types of sentences much.	❑ The tone is somewhat informal. ❑ The language is not very strong or persuasive.
1 Huh?	❑ The writing does not sound real or unique. I do not know who the writer is. ❑ The sentences are not interesting.	❑ The tone is too informal. ❑ The writer does not use strong language.

Name _____ Date _____

Writing Project

Author's Viewpoint Chart

Complete the chart for your editorial.

Claim	Facts or other support	Action needed

Unit 6 | Food for Thought

Name _____   Date _____

Writing Project

Revise

Use revision marks to make changes to these paragraphs. Look for:

- persuasive language
- clear reasons supported by relevant evidence
- a formal tone and writing that does not include contractions
- different lengths and types of sentences

Revision Marks	
∧	Add
⌒	Take out
∧̢	Insert comma
⌒⌒	Move to here

Poison for Breakfast

What's your favorite breakfast cereal? If you eat Fruity Crunch Fluffs, you might want to stop.

The extra sugar, colors, and artificial flavors in Fruity Crunch Fluffs aren't good for you. The sugar makes you gain weight and affects your teeth. The fake colors and flavors are created with chemicals that can cause cancer when consumed in high amounts, according to some studies.

Also, Fruity Crunch Fluffs are made with genetically modified corn. We don't really know how bad GMs are, Maybe they're not so bad. I think people should avoid Fruity Crunch Fluffs.

Name _____ Date _____

Writing Project

Edit and Proofread

Use revision marks to edit and proofread these paragraphs. Look for:

- correct use of reflexive and intensive pronouns
- correct use of subject and object pronouns
- correct spelling of homophones

Revision Marks	
∧	Add
⌿	Take out
⊙	Insert period
=	Capitalize
/	Make lowercase

Poison for Breakfast (continued)

I myselves prefer to eat only cereal that is maid with organic ingredients. This means that the corn was not sprayed with chemicals. I learned this from my aunt, who is a farmer. Her says that if you do not no where something was groan, you should not eat them. My aunt itself grows only organic crops on her farm.

Us should always ask ourself wear our food comes from. Breakfast is the most important meal of the day, so do not skip him. Make sure you feed you're body something better than Fruity Crunch Fluffs!

Name _____ Date _____

Unit Concept Map

Ancient China

Make a concept map with the answers to the Big Question:
Why should we study ancient cultures?

Why should we study ancient cultures?		
What I <u>know</u>	What I <u>want</u> to know	What I <u>learned</u>

Name _____ Date _____

Thinking Map

Relate Ideas

Complete the text evidence chart about a historical figure you have studied.

Person's qualities	Text evidence

With a partner, choose a historical figure you have studied. Take turns identifying qualities that describe the person. Then relate ideas and text evidence that demonstrate those qualities.

Name _____ Date _____

Grammar

Vague Pronouns: Fix the Sentences

Read each pair of sentences. Circle the pronouns that do not have a clear antecedent and rewrite the sentences to fix the problem.

1. Marco took a photograph of John. He made a silly face.

   _____

   _____

2. John showed the photo to Hector. He laughed.

   _____

   _____

3. Penny gave Maria an apple. She loved apples.

   _____

   _____

4. Maria put the apple in a bag. It was green.

   _____

   _____

5. Maria and Penny saw the boys at the food stand. They were surprised.

   _____

   _____

7.3   Unit 7 | Ancient China

Key Points Reading

"The Emperor's Silent Army"

Listen as your teacher reads. Follow with your finger.

1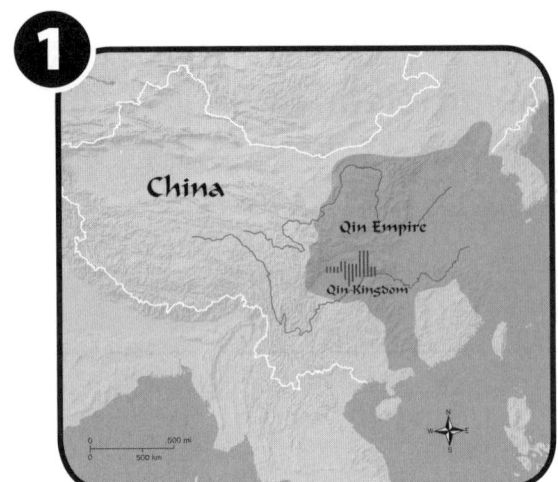

Once, there was no China. Instead, there were seven kingdoms. They had been fighting one another for hundreds of years. The king of Qin and his army ruled the fiercest kingdom.

By 221 B.C., the king of Qin had conquered the other kingdoms. He combined them into one empire. He chose a new title in honor of his conquest, Qin Shihuang. This means "first emperor, God in Heaven, and Almighty of the Universe."

2

The only thing Qin Shihuang feared was death. He wanted to live forever. He ate powdered jade and drank mercury to lengthen his life. In fact, these things probably caused his death.

Qin Shihuang died while on a tour of his empire. Fearing a revolt, his ministers kept the emperor's death a secret. They pretended Qin Shihuang was alive and kept his body hidden in his chariot until they safely reached the capital city.

Key Points Reading

"The Emperor's Silent Army" (continued)

3

Qin Shihuang's tomb was larger than his largest palace and richly decorated. Pearls were arranged on the ceiling to look like the sun, moon, and stars. The floor was made of bronze. It showed a map of the world with rivers of mercury and replicas of mountains, palaces, and cities.

Weapons were placed inside the tomb to protect the treasures. These included mechanical bows that would shoot arrows at intruders.

4

Archaeologists know of Qin Shihuang's tomb from ancient Chinese records. However, the records don't mention the terracotta army that guarded the tomb. Over 6,000 clay soldiers and horses were buried in pits surrounding the tomb.

The largest pit shows the soldiers standing ready for battle. The archers stand in front of the foot soldiers. Amid these soldiers are charioteers and teams of horses. The soldiers in the side columns and at the rear face outward, prepared for an attack from any direction.

Name _____ Date _____

Grammar

Missing Antecedents

Read the sentences. Circle the pronouns that are missing an antecedent. Then rewrite the sentences to fix the problem.

1. Yesterday, I went to the library. They can help you find books there.

   _____
   _____

2. I am writing about Chinese emperors. It is due on Monday.

   _____
   _____

3. My teacher visited China. She showed us pictures from her trip.

   _____
   _____

4. Beijing is a busy city in China. They ride their bicycles everywhere.

   _____
   _____

5. It was five o' clock when I got home. I told them about what I had learned.

   _____
   _____

Name _____   Date _____

Reread and Retell

"The Emperor's Silent Army"

Complete the text evidence chart about Qin Shihuang.

Person's qualities	Text evidence
brutal, mean	Qin Shihuang's soldiers had to cut off their enemies' heads.

List Qin Shihuang's qualities and the text evidence that demonstrates these qualities. Use the completed chart to analyze with a partner why Qin Shihuang was a key figure in Chinese history.

7.7   Unit 7 | Ancient China

Fluency

"The Emperor's Silent Army"

Use this passage to practice reading with proper phrasing.

If word of Qin Shihuang's death got out while he was away from	13
the capital there might be a revolt. So his ministers kept the news a	27
secret. With the emperor's body inside his chariot, the entire party	38
traveled back to the capital city. Meals were brought into the emperor's	50
chariot; daily reports on affairs of state were delivered as usual—all to	63
keep up the appearance that the emperor was alive and well. However,	75
it was summer, and a terrible smell began to come from the chariot. But	89
the clever ministers found a way to account for the stench. A cart was	103
loaded with smelly, salted fish and made to precede the chariot,	114
overpowering and masking any foul odors coming from the dead	124
emperor. And so Qin Shihuang returned to the capital for burial.	135

From "The Emperor's Silent Army," page 165

Phrasing
- 1 ☐ Rarely pauses while reading the text.
- 2 ☐ Occasionally pauses while reading the text.
- 3 ☐ Frequently pauses at appropriate points in the text.
- 4 ☐ Consistently pauses at all appropriate points in the text.

Accuracy and Rate Formula
Use the formula to measure a reader's accuracy and rate while reading aloud.

_____ − _____ = _____
words attempted   number of errors   words correct per minute
in one minute   (wcpm)

Name _____ Date _____

Reading Options

"A Silent Army"

List three interesting facts you read about in the history article.

That's a Fact!

One interesting fact I read is _____ _____ _____.
Another interesting fact I read is _____ _____ _____.
One more interesting fact I read is _____ _____ _____.

 Tell a partner which fact was most interesting and why.

7.9

Name _____ Date _____

Respond and Extend

Compare Details

Complete the comparison chart to compare details in the two reading selections.

	"The Emperor's Silent Army"	"A Silent Army"
History of Qin Shihuang's Life	Details:	Details: • ruled about 2,200 years ago
Qin Shihuang's Tomb	Details:	Details:
Qin's Terracotta Army	Details	Details

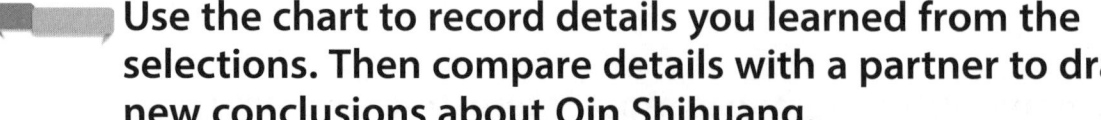 Use the chart to record details you learned from the selections. Then compare details with a partner to draw new conclusions about Qin Shihuang.

7.10 Unit 7 | Ancient China

Name _____ Date _____

Grammar

The Emperor's Tomb

Grammar Rules Pronoun Agreement

1. A **pronoun** must agree with its antecedent in number and person.

2. Use a **subject pronoun** as the **subject** of a sentence.
   - The **singular** subject pronouns are **I, you, he, she**, and **it**.
   - The **plural** subject pronouns are **we, you**, and **they**.

3. Use an **object pronoun** after an <u>action verb</u> or a <u>preposition</u>.
   - The **singular** object pronouns are **me, you, him, her**, and **it**.
   - The **plural** object pronouns are **us, you**, and **them**.

Read each sentence or pair of sentences. Write the correct pronoun on the blank. Then circle its antecedent.

1. The tomb is near the excavation pits. _____ is still intact.

2. Archaeologists know where the tomb is, but _____ have not found the entrance.

3. Some people want the emperor to rest in peace. These people do not want to disturb _____ by opening the tomb.

4. Conservationists are worried about damaging the artifacts. It is up to _____ to protect the valuable pieces.

5. Jacqueline Ball helped write the article. _____ says the conservationists are figuring out how to protect the artifacts.

▸ Tell a partner what you learned about Qin Shihuang. Use subject and object pronouns. Ask your partner to check for pronoun agreement and clear antecedents.

Name _____ Date _____

Close Reading

from "A Silent Army," pages 177–178

Analyze the text below with your teacher and make notes.

1   It was 1974. In Xi'an, 930 km (580 miles) southwest of Beijing, some farmers were digging a well. Reaching a level of 4.6 meters (15 feet) below ground, they uncovered a fragment of pottery that looked like the head of a very large sculpture of a man. The farmers could tell right away that this pottery was more important than finishing the well. They told a local official, who instantly called in archaeologists.

2   Working like crime scene investigators, the archaeologists carefully excavated the area around the farmers' well. They found many statues of soldiers made of a red clay called terracotta. They also found clay horses and chariots. It was as if a whole army lay beneath the earth. The site is only a mile from the main tomb of the First Emperor of China, Qin Shihuang, who lived from 259 B.C. to 201 B.C. They knew this massive group of sculptures must be part of his tomb complex.

Name _____   Date _____

Close Reading

from "A Silent Army," page 183

Make notes as you read the paragraphs below. Then answer the questions on page 7.14.

1. Archaeologists are still digging up terracotta soldiers. In fact, in the 30 years since the army was discovered, only 1,000 of the estimated 8,000 soldiers have been uncovered. But the terracotta army is also one of the most popular tourist destinations in China. It is facing a dangerous, modern enemy. In the 1990s, the Chinese government erected enormous buildings over the dig site to protect the warriors from the weather. They also allowed 1.5 million visitors each year to come and watch the ongoing excavation.

2. But the site is in Xi'an, which is one of the most polluted cities in the world. In addition, all those visitors breathing in a closed building have added a lot of moisture to the air. The moisture got so bad that mold has grown on many of the statues.

Name _____ Date _____

Close Reading

from "A Silent Army" (continued)

Reread and annotate the passage to answer these questions.

Reread paragraph 1.

1. Draw a conclusion about how long it will take archaeologists to excavate every single part of the terracotta army. Highlight text evidence that helped you draw your conclusion.

2. How do people in China feel about the terracotta army? How do you know? Highlight text evidence that supports your answer.

Reread paragraph 2.

3. Identify details that support the idea that the terracotta army is "facing a dangerous, modern enemy." Highlight these details within the text.

4. What is the main idea of the passage? Record your main idea in the margin at the end of the paragraph.

Name _____   Date _____

Thinking Map

Elements of Fiction

Complete the double plot diagram.

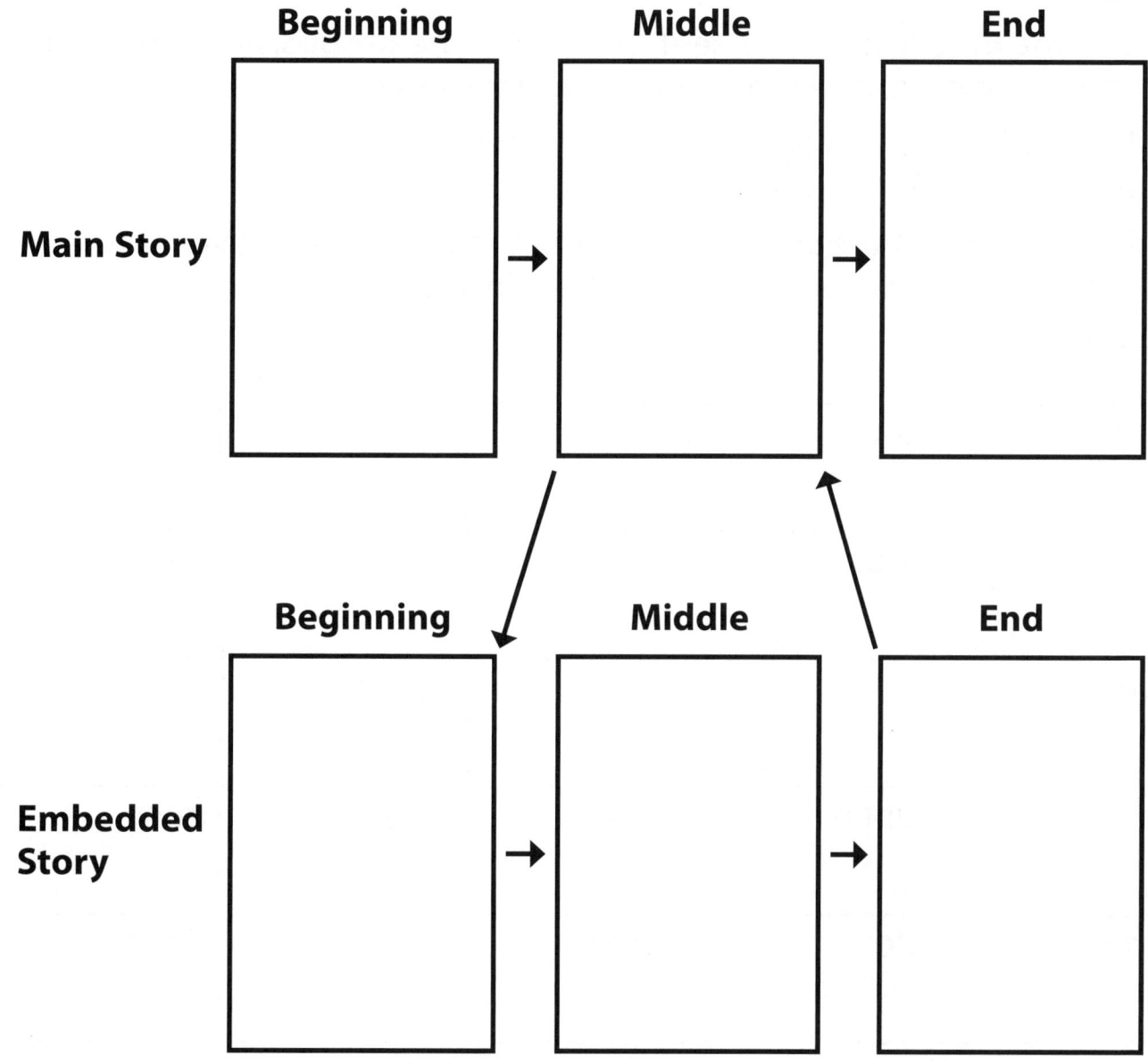

Tell a partner about an important day in your life, and explain the events as the main story. Tell an embedded story that gives more background information. Have your partner fill in the diagram to record your stories.

Name _____ Date _____

Grammar

Points for Prepositional Phrases

1. Play with three or four people. Take turns.
2. Toss your marker onto a square. Read the **preposition** on it.
3. Use the **preposition** in a sentence. Tell if the **prepositional phrase** shows location, direction, time, or other details.
4. If the other players agree with you, put your initials in the space. If not, do not write your initials.
5. Play until all of the spaces have initials in them. The player whose initials are in the most spaces is the winner.

over	down	before	below	next to
to	around	between	among	through
under	up	against	out of	until
on	during	behind	along	from
across	into	beside	across	after
at	for	of	with	without

7.16 Unit 7 | Ancient China

Key Points Reading

"Where the Mountain Meets the Moon"

Listen as your teacher reads. Follow with your finger.

1

Every day, Minli and her parents work in the muddy rice fields. It is tiring work, and still the family is poor and has little to eat. Minli wishes she could change her family's fortune. Just then, a man appears selling goldfish. When he says goldfish bring fortune to a home, Minli buys one.

2

Ma is upset that Minli spent her money on a goldfish. Ba tries to make Minli feel better by saying maybe the fish will bring them fortune, but Ma disagrees. When Minli asks what *will* bring them fortune, Ba says that is a question for the Old Man of the Moon. Minli begs Ba to tell her the story, and he does.

3

Once there was a powerful magistrate who was very proud. He demanded that everyone bow to him or be punished. One night, the magistrate saw an old man reading a large book and holding a bag of red string. Angry that the old man didn't bow, the magistrate demanded to know what he was reading.

Name _____ Date _____

Key Points Reading

"Where the Mountain Meets the Moon" (continued)

4

The old man said it was the Book of Fortune which could answer any question. When asked who the magistrate's son would marry, the old man revealed that it would be a grocer's daughter. He had tied their futures together with his red string. The magistrate was angry because he wanted his son to marry royalty, so he sent a servant to kill the girl.

5

Years later, the magistrate's son married one of the emperor's granddaughters. He asked his new wife why she wore a flower on her forehead. She explained that the flower hid a scar where she had been stabbed. Her father had been a grocer, but the emperor's son adopted her after her family died.

6

Hearing the story, Minli wants to find the old man and ask how to bring fortune to her house. She regrets buying the goldfish and decides to release it into the river. That night, she is surprised to hear the goldfish speak. It thanks her for releasing it and tells her how to find the Old Man of the Moon.

Name _____   Date _____

Grammar

Prepositional Phrase Scramble

Unscramble the words in each row to make a **prepositional phrase**. Write the phrase on the line.

1. stone   wall   by   the   _____

2. morning   on   sunny   a   _____

3. voice   loud   a   in   _____

4. distant   a   from   town   _____

5. price   good   a   for   _____

Choose a phrase from above to expand each sentence. Follow the directions in parentheses. Use correct capitalization and punctuation. Then trade papers with a partner and check each other's sentences.

1. _____ a trader visited the village. (tell "when")

2. He came _____. (tell "where")

3. He set up his cart _____. (tell "where")

4. _____ the trader announced what he had for sale. (tell "how")

5. He said, "I am selling hats and coats _____." (tell "how")

Name _____ Date _____

Vocabulary

Vocabulary Bingo

Play Bingo using the Key Words from this unit.

7.20   Unit 7 | Ancient China

Name _____ Date _____

Reread and Retell

"Where the Mountain Meets the Moon"

Use the double plot diagram to record events from "Where the Mountain Meets the Moon."

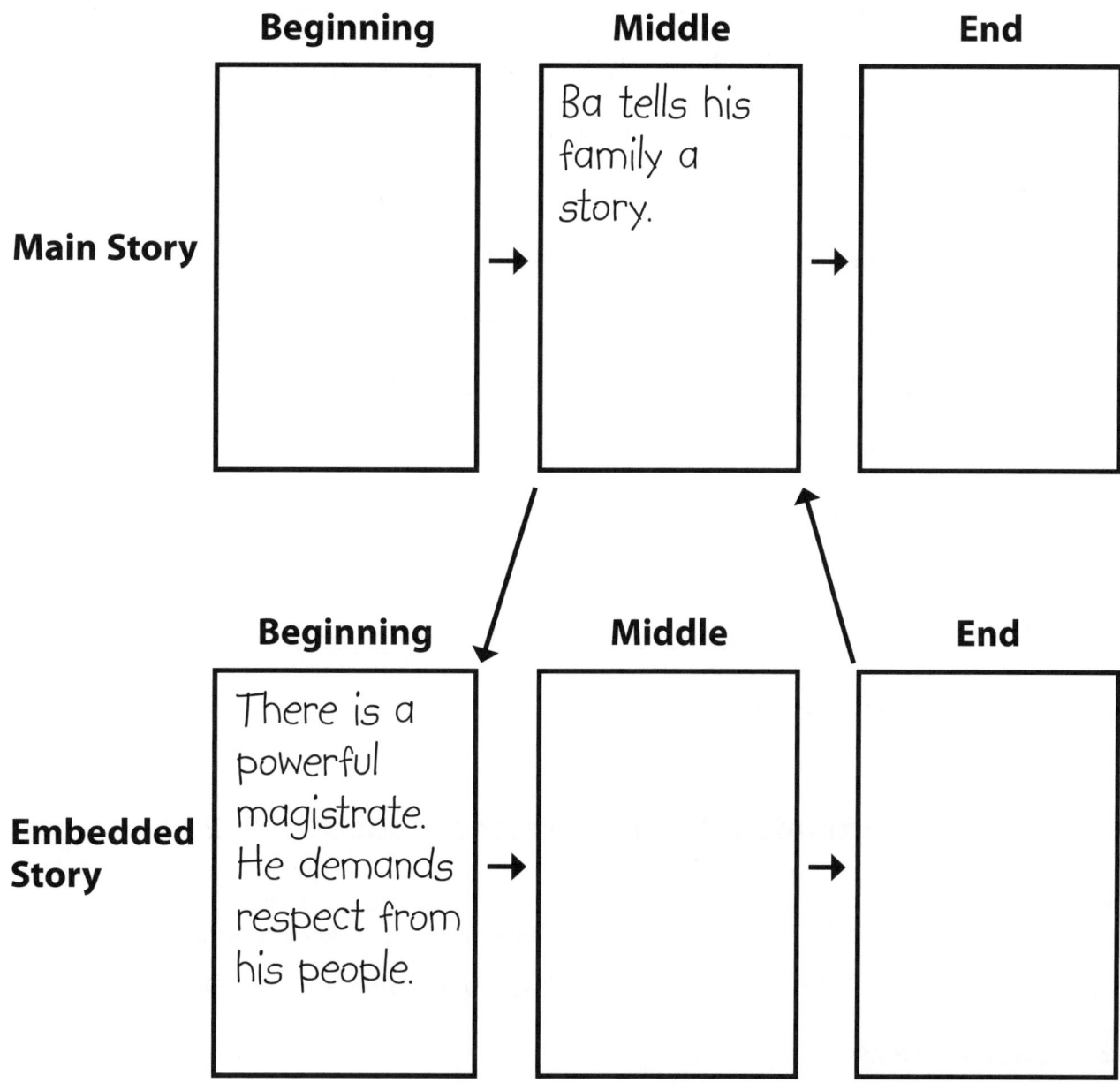

Main Story

Beginning:

Middle: Ba tells his family a story.

End:

Embedded Story

Beginning: There is a powerful magistrate. He demands respect from his people.

Middle:

End:

Complete the double plot diagram. Use the diagram to tell a partner the story summaries and explain how the embedded story relates to the plot of the main story.

7.21

Unit 7 | Ancient China

Name _____ Date _____

Fluency

"Where the Mountain Meets the Moon"

Use this passage to practice reading with proper expression.

Once there was a magistrate who was quite powerful and	10
proud. He was so proud that he demanded constant respect from	21
his people. Whenever he made a trip out of the city, no matter	34
what time of day or night, people were to leave their homes, get	47
on their knees, and make deep bows as he passed, or else face	60
the brutal punishment of his soldiers. The magistrate was fierce	70
in his anger as well as his pride. It is said he even expected the	85
monkeys to come down from the trees to bow to him.	96
The magistrate was harsh with his subordinates, ruthless to	105
his enemies, and pitiless to his people. All feared his wrath, and	117
when he roared his orders the people trembled. Behind his back,	128
they called him Magistrate Tiger.	133

From "Where the Mountain Meets the Moon," pages 199–200

Expression
- 1 ☐ Does not read with feeling.
- 2 ☐ Reads with some feeling but does not match content.
- 3 ☐ Reads with appropriate feeling for most content.
- 4 ☐ Reads with appropriate feeling for all content.

Accuracy and Rate Formula
Use the formula to measure a reader's accuracy and rate while reading aloud.

_____ − _____ = _____
words attempted in one minute | number of errors | words correct per minute (wcpm)

7.22   Unit 7 | Ancient China

Name _____   Date _____

Reading Options

"Mu Lan: The Girl Who Knew No Fear"

Complete the chart as you read the play.

Page	What I read	What it means to me

▶ Tell a partner which detail was most interesting and why.

Name _____ Date _____

Respond and Extend

Compare Experiences

Complete the comparison chart.

Title	Reading experience	Viewing and listening experience
"Where the Mountain Meets the Moon"	• • •	• • •
"Mu Lan: The Girl Who Knew No Fear"	• Sometimes, it was hard to read because of the character names and play directions. • •	• • •

 Discuss with a partner how reading a story is different from listening to or viewing the same story. Write your ideas in the comparison chart.

Name _____   Date _____

Grammar

Mu Lan, a Brave Soldier

Grammar Rules: Prepositional Phrases

Use prepositional phrases to:
- show location.   *Mu Lan camped **near** the mountain.*
- show direction. *The enemy could come **down** the hill.*
- show time.   ***After** dinner, Mu Lan shared her plan.*
- give details.   *Some laughed **at** Mu Lan's idea.*

Expand each sentence with a prepositional phrase.

1. Mu Lan lived in a small village _____.

2. She learned how to ride a horse _____.

3. When invaders came, Mu Lan became a soldier _____.

4. She tricked the invaders by sending goats _____.

5. The invaders stopped fighting and sent a message _____.

6. Everyone thought Mu Lan was the bravest and most skillful soldier _____.

Tell a partner something you learned about China by reading about Mu Lan. Use prepositional phrases in your sentences.

7.25

Unit 7 | Ancient China

Name _____ Date _____

Close Reading

from "Mu Lan: The Girl Who Knew No Fear," page 214

Analyze the text below with your teacher and make notes.

1. **NARRATOR 1:** Long ago, when many an ancient story was as new as the first grass in spring, there lived a girl named Mu Lan.

2. **NARRATOR 2:** She lived in a quiet village in China, where farmers' fields spread out in all directions like embroidered cloths of green and gold. No star in the heavens was ever as brilliant as Mu Lan.

3. **NARRATOR 1:** From the time that she was a child, Mu Lan demonstrated a tremendous capacity for learning. With her quick wit and her restless wonder, Mu Lan could follow a line of thought, no matter how complex, as easily as a bird in flight distinguishes its invisible path. She admired new ideas the way some people admire a beautiful sunrise.

4. **NARRATOR 2:** Picture her now as she was then.

5. [FATHER *and* MOTHER *enter. They are proud of* MU LAN.]

6. **FATHER:** Mu Lan, your mother and I are pleased with your devotion to your studies. You behave with respect to your teachers, and you work tirelessly at your lessons. So we were wondering—

7. **MOTHER:** Now that you have learned to read and write, to recite our history, and to map many lands—

8. **FATHER:** What would you like to study next?

Name _____ Date _____

Close Reading

from "Mu Lan: The Girl Who Knew No Fear," pages 221–222

Make notes as you read the paragraphs below. Then answer the questions on page 7.28.

1. **GENERAL HUA:** Commanding Officer, I'm afraid I don't see how your strategy can help us.

2. **MESSENGER:** No one is afraid of goats!

3. [MESSENGER and SOLDIERS *start to laugh*.]

4. **SOLDIER 1:** In this dark, I cannot even see the goats, only the glow of the lanterns.

5. **SOLDIER 2:** [*more and more amused*] Why, for all that the enemy knows, those goats could just be soldiers . . .

6. **SOLDIER 1:** Yes, from here they resemble nothing so much as soldiers, each one holding up a lantern.

7. **MESSENGER:** [*giggling*] Just like hundreds and hundreds of soldiers moving up the mountain.

8. **GENERAL HUA:** Now I understand your strategy!

9. [ALL *stop laughing*.]

10. **NARRATOR 1:** Sure enough, when the enemy saw the lanterns move up the cliff, they came to the conclusion—a false conclusion—that General Hua's army was attacking.

Name _____   Date _____

Close Reading

from "Mu Lan: The Girl Who Knew No Fear" (continued)

Reread and annotate the passage to answer these questions.

Reread paragraphs 1–5.

1. How do the messenger and the soldiers respond to Mu Lan's strategy for fighting against the enemy's army? Highlight text evidence.

2. Describe how the strategy is working. Highlight text evidence that supports your answer.

Reread paragraph 6–10.

3. General Hua says: "Now I understand your strategy!" What does he understand? How does the strategy work? Highlight text evidence.

4. How is this scene the beginning of a turning point in the play's plot?

Name _____   Date _____

Writing Project

Ideas

Writing is well-developed when the message is clear and interesting to the reader. It is supported by details that show the writer knows the topic well.

	Does the story have a clear central conflict?	**Are the characters, plot, and setting well-developed?**
4 Wow!	❏ The story has a clear central conflict. ❏ The conflict is resolved at the end in a satisfying way.	❏ The characters are strong and interesting. ❏ The writing includes descriptive details to develop the characters, plot, and setting.
3 Ahh.	❏ The story has a fairly clear central conflict. ❏ The conflict is mostly resolved at the end.	❏ The characters are fairly strong and interesting. ❏ The writing includes some descriptive details to develop the characters, plot, and setting.
2 Hmm.	❏ The story has a central conflict, but it is not very clear. ❏ The conflict is only partly resolved.	❏ The characters are not that strong or interesting. ❏ The writer uses only a few details to develop the characters, plot, and setting.
1 Huh?	❏ The story is missing a central conflict. ❏ The ending is not satisfying.	❏ The characters are not interesting. ❏ The writing does not include enough details.

Name _____ Date _____

Writing Project

Character Chart

Complete the character chart for your story.

Character	Motivation	Actions	Traits

Name _____ Date _____

Writing Project

Revise

Use revision marks to make changes to these paragraphs. Look for places to:

- develop characters by using more precise words
- add descriptive details about the setting and plot
- add transitions that connect ideas and events

Revision Marks	
^	Add
℘	Take out
⌄	Insert comma
/	Make lowercase

The Fox and the Raven

There was a fox who lived in a forest. He was always tricking other animals to get what he wanted.

The fox saw a raven on the branch of a tree. She was carrying a piece of meat in her beak. The fox was really hungry and wanted the meat. So he spoke to the raven and said nice things to her. He told her she had beautiful black feathers and a strong voice. He said she was brave. He even called her the queen of all birds.

The raven swelled with pride and said, "Thank you! Thank you!" When she opened her beak, the meat fell to the ground. The fox picked it up and ate it. Then he left.

Writing Project

Edit and Proofread

Use revision marks to edit and proofread these paragraphs. Look for:

- correct use of pronouns
- clear antecedents
- correct forms of contractions

Editing Marks	
∧	Add
℘	Take out
⸝∧	Insert apostrophe

The Fox and the Raven Meet Again

The raven, queen of all birds, was soaring through the forest one day when they spotted the fox down below. He was caught in a hunter's trap.

"Raven, my old friend!" he cried out to her. "Please help me! Im stuck in this trap, and he will be coming back any minute. Youre my only hope."

"Hah!" she replied. "You ain't going to trick me again. The other animals and I are tired of your games."

"No, I promise its not a trick!" said the fox.

"Sorry, but when we doesn't treat others kindly, you get what you deserve." And with that, the raven flew off.

Name _____ Date _____

Unit Concept Map

Earth and Beyond

Make a concept map with the answers to the Big Question: How does studying Earth tell us about other planets?

- Some planets are made of rock and metal, just like Earth.
- Some planets have volcanoes like Earth does.

How does studying Earth tell us about other planets?

Name _____   Date _____

Thinking Map

Compare and Contrast

Complete the comparison-contrast chart.

	Place 1 Beach	Place 2 Mountains	Comparison or contrast

Describe two places as a partner writes the information in the chart. Work together to write a statement that is true about both places.

Name _____   Date _____

Grammar

Ways to Join Sentences

Grammar Rules Compound Sentences and Conjunctions

1. A **compound sentence** contains two complete sentences joined by a comma and a **conjunction**.
2. The conjunction **and** joins two similar ideas.
3. The conjunction **but** joins two different ideas or shows contrast.
4. The conjunction **or** joins two choices.
5. The conjunction **so** shows cause and effect.

Read each pair of sentences. Use them to write a compound sentence with a conjunction. Use each conjunction only once.

1. Mars and Earth have similar features. The two planets are very different.
   _____
   _____

2. The surface of Mars is a red rock. Mars is sometimes called the Red Planet.
   _____
   _____

3. My sister knows a lot about Mars. She is learning about other planets.
   _____
   _____

4. Someday she may be an astronaut. She may become a teacher.
   _____
   _____

Key Points Reading

"Finding Mars on Earth"

Listen as your teacher reads. Follow with your finger.

1

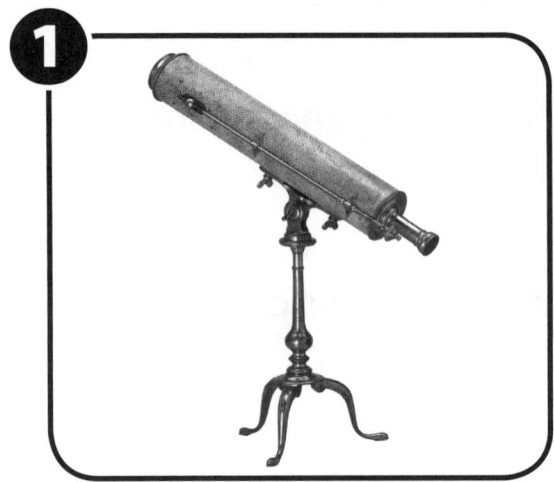

When astronomers first looked at Mars through telescopes, they saw white masses and thought of polar ice caps on Earth. They also saw curving lines and thought of canals people had built on Earth.

In 1971, a space probe called *Mariner 9* got close to Mars. It took pictures that showed volcanoes, canyons, and ice caps. Since then, scientists have learned a lot about Mars.

2

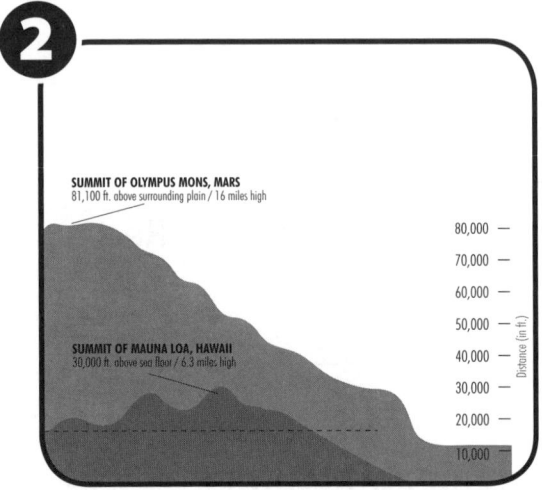

Scientists study pictures from Mars and compare them to similar geologic features on Earth. Scientists have learned that Mars has a volcano. Olympus Mons is a shield volcano, just like Mauna Loa in Hawaii. Scientists used what they know about shield volcanoes to infer that Olympus Mons has a hotspot beneath it. The hotspot contains magma.

Key Points Reading

"Finding Mars on Earth" (continued)

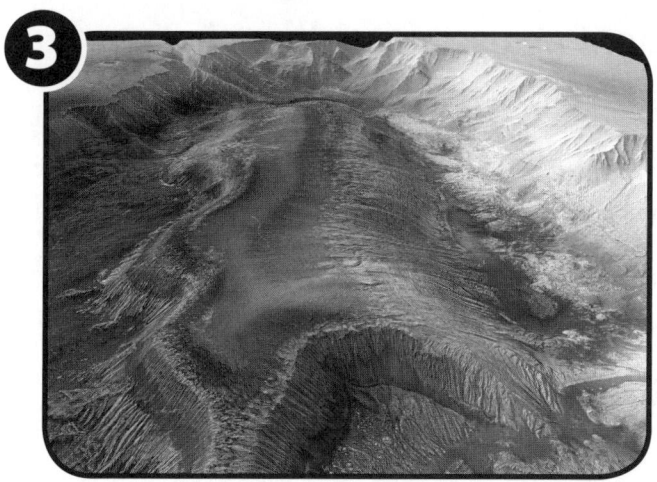

③

Valles Marineris is a canyon on Mars. It resembles the Grand Canyon in the United States. It has steep sides with a channel in between. The Colorado River helped shape the Grand Canyon. Could an ancient Martian river have helped to form Hebes Chasma? If Mars once had water, did it also have life? These are some of the many questions scientists are trying to answer.

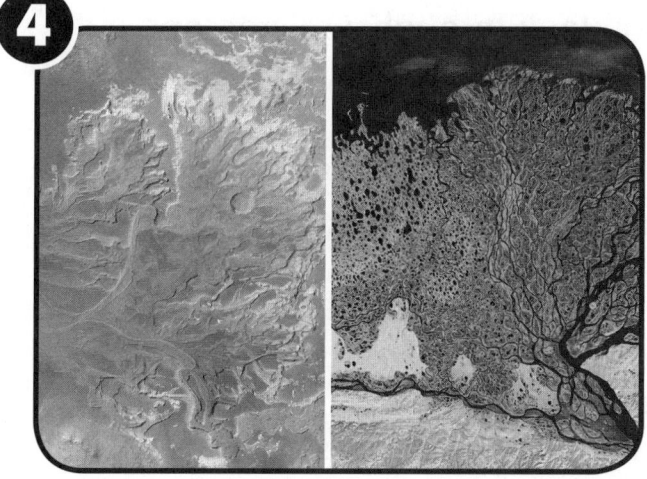

④

Earth and Mars have many similar features. That suggests that water also helped shape the landforms on Mars. There are features that look like river deltas and craters on Earth that formed from dried up lakes. Mars also has "blueberries," or hematite mineral balls, that are known to form near hot springs.

Still, scientists are cautious about making too many comparisons. They know that each feature could have formed in other ways. We still have much to learn about Mars.

Name _____   Date _____

Grammar

Make Complex Sentences

1. Make word cards. Put the independent clauses face down in one set. Put the dependent clauses face down in another set.
2. Take turns drawing a clause from each set. If you can, join the two clauses to make a complex sentence that is true. Tell a partner how you would correctly write the sentence.
3. If your partner agrees that you are correct, you get one point.
4. If you cannot make a sentence, return one clause face down to the correct set and draw a new clause from that set. If you still can't make a sentence, your partner takes a turn.
5. Play until all the strips have been joined.

Independent clauses	Dependent clauses
the terrains of Earth and Mars are uneven	if you look through a microscope
you will see microorganisms in Earth's soil	because scientists now use powerful telescopes
the days on Mars and Earth are about the same length	before the rovers went there
people can see more details of planets and other objects	since Earth and Mars spin at about the same rate
we knew little about Mars	after they take pictures and gather samples
rovers send information to scientists on Earth	because they are made of rock and metal

8.6

Unit 8 | Earth and Beyond

Name _____   Date _____

Reread and Retell

"Finding Mars on Earth"

Use the comparison-contrast chart to review "Finding Mars on Earth."

	Mauna Loa Volcano	Olympus Mons Volcano	Comparison or contrast
Location	Hawaii, Earth	Mars	Both planets have volcanoes.
Type	shield volcano		
Temperature			
Height			
Width			
Gravity			

💬 With a partner, take turns listing details about a geologic feature found on both Earth and Mars. Work together to synthesize the information to form a generalization about the feature.

8.7

Unit 8 | Earth and Beyond

Name _____ Date _____

Fluency

"Finding Mars on Earth"

Use this passage to practice reading with proper intonation.

Where there is water, there is life. We know that is true on	13
Earth. So if there were rivers on ancient Mars, does that mean	25
there was life there, as well? (And could that life still be there	38
now?) Those are questions scientists are trying to answer, and	48
one of their most important sources of information is craters.	58
If you have ever punched your fist into the sand, then you	70
already understand a lot about one kind of crater—the impact	81
crater. Impact craters are simply low areas created by the	91
impact of objects from space.	96
Impact craters are like ponds or lakes—they are natural, low	107
places for water to settle and be contained. And just like in ponds and	121
lakes, naturally occurring materials from the environment, called	129
sediments, sink to the bottoms of crater lakes.	137

From "Finding Mars on Earth," page 250

Intonation
- [1] ☐ Does not change pitch.
- [2] ☐ Changes pitch but does not match content.
- [3] ☐ Changes pitch to match some of the content.
- [4] ☐ Changes pitch to match all of the content.

Accuracy and Rate Formula
Use the formula to measure a reader's accuracy and rate while reading aloud.

_____ − _____ = _____
words attempted   number of errors   words correct per minute
  in one minute   (wcpm)

8.8

Unit 8 | Earth and Beyond

Name _____ Date _____

Reading Options

"Here, There, and Beyond"

List three amazing facts you read about in the science article.

That's amazing!

An amazing fact about _____

is _____.

It is amazing because _____

_____.

That's amazing!

An amazing fact about _____

is _____.

It is amazing because _____

_____.

That's amazing!

An amazing fact about _____

is _____.

It is amazing because _____

_____.

🗨️ Tell a partner which fact was your favorite and why.

Name _____ Date _____

Respond and Extend

Compare Information

Complete the comparison chart.

	Examples in "Finding Mars on Earth"	Examples in "Here, There, and Beyond"	How features give information
Text	descriptions of geologic features		
Photos and captions		photos of planets and space objects	
Charts			
Diagrams			

Use the chart to record how information is presented in each text and its text features. Then discuss with a partner how these features help you understand the topic.

Name _____ Date _____

Grammar

Space Exploration

Grammar Rules Compound and Complex Sentences

1. A **compound sentence** combines two **independent clauses**.
2. To form a compound sentence, use a comma plus the **conjunction** **and**, **or**, **but**, or **so** to join the **independent clauses**.
3. A **complex sentence** combines an **independent clause** and one or more **dependent clauses**. A dependent clause begins with a **subordinating conjunction**, such as **because**, **if**, **before**, or **since**.
4. To form a complex sentence, you can put the dependent clause first or last. If you put it first, put a comma after it.

Read each sentence. Draw one line under each independent clause and two lines under each dependent clause. Then write **compound** or **complex** to identify the sentence type.

1. Telescopes are necessary even in space because astronauts cannot easily see far away without them.
2. Some of the telescopes look at close objects, but others look far into the distant galaxy.
3. Since space telescopes are far above Earth, they are not affected by bright city lights.
4. Astronauts go on spacewalks when telescopes need repairs.
5. Telescope parts can be damaged in space, so astronauts always bring extra parts from Earth.

_____ Tell a partner what you learned about exploring our solar system. Use some compound and complex sentences. Ask your partner to identify these sentences.

8.11   Unit 8 | Earth and Beyond

Grammar

Combine the Clauses

1. Make cards and place them face down in a pile.
2. Take turns with a partner. Turn over one card from the pile.
3. Read the two clauses on your card. If your card is white, combine the clauses into a compound sentence. If your card is gray, combine the clauses into a complex sentence.
4. Write the new sentence on the back of your card. Add any needed conjunction, punctuation, or capitalization.
5. If your partner agrees that the sentence is correct, you get one point.
6. The first player to get five points is the winner.

Harry fished Hans sailed the raft	the sea lizard flipped the raft the crocodile chomped it
the clouds became darker thunder sounded in the distance	Harry was eager to cross the sea he was nervous
Harry's uncle finished speaking Harry was worried	the island had a huge geyser they decided to keep sailing
Harry wanted to stop exploring Harry's uncle kept advancing	the explorers set sail Hans finished building the raft

Name _____ Date _____

Close Reading

from "Here, There, and Beyond," pages 262-263

Analyze the text below with your teacher and make notes.

1. The four planets closest to the sun—Mercury, Venus, Earth, and Mars—have a lot in common. They are mostly made of rock and metal, so they all have hard, uneven terrains. Because of their compositions, the planets closest to the sun have high densities. This means that these planets are made of condensed, or tightly packed, materials.

2. In addition to sharing common structural features, the rocky planets closest to the sun are alike in other ways. They are small in comparison to most other planets in our solar system, and they have fewer moons. They also share the quality of having short "years" with relatively quick revolutions around the sun.

3. Even though they have many similarities, each of these four planets differs individually from the others in its group. For example, each planet has a different kind of atmosphere. An atmosphere is a blanket of gas that covers a planet. Mercury has almost no atmosphere, and both Venus and Mars have atmospheres that are mainly carbon dioxide. Earth's atmosphere is primarily nitrogen and oxygen.

Name _____   Date _____

Close Reading

from "Here, There, and Beyond," page 264

Make notes as you read the paragraphs below. Then answer the questions on page 8.15.

1. The next group of four planets is Jupiter, Saturn, Uranus, and Neptune. These planets are huge in comparison to the first group. Unlike the planets closer to the sun, these planets do not have compositions of rock or other solid matter. They lack solid, well-defined surfaces. Their atmospheres are mostly made of gases, so many scientists call these planets "gas giants."

2. Gas giants have many moons and rings that are made of dust and rocks. The rings of some gas giants are difficult to see, while those of other planets, such as Saturn, are visible from Earth.

3. Although the gas giants share many similarities, each planet is unique. Some of the gas giants have storms on their surfaces. For example, the orange-red oval shown on Jupiter is a storm that has lasted more than 300 years.

4. Gas giants can also move through space in different ways. Uranus spins on its side, like a rolling ball instead of a spinning top. It is the only planet in our solar system that spins this way.

Name _____ Date _____

Close Reading

from "Here, There, and Beyond" (continued)

Reread and annotate the passage to answer these questions.

Reread paragraphs 1–2.

1. Which planets is the author talking about in this section of the article? Highlight text evidence that gives a clue about where these planets are located in our solar system.

2. Why are these planets known as "gas giants"? Highlight text evidence that supports your answer.

Reread paragraphs 3–4.

3. Summarize information about Jupiter's storm in your own words. Highlight text evidence that helped you with your summary.

4. The author says that each gas giant is "unique." Explain how Uranus is unique. Highlight text evidence.

Name _____ Date _____

Thinking Map

Word Choice

Use the word choice chart to describe a school or community event.

Story language	What the words describe	Mood	Impact on reader

▸ **Choose specific, vivid words to describe a school or community event in a way that will make a partner feel happy about it. Have your partner complete the chart based on your description. Then complete a chart as your partner describes the same event to create a different mood.**

Name _____   Date _____

Grammar

Make Sentences Flow

Read each pair of sentences. Condense them into one sentence by combining ideas. Write the new sentence on the line.

1. This book was written by a man. He had a great imagination.
   _____
   _____

2. Lourdes likes to read science fiction. Maddie likes to read science fiction, too.
   _____
   _____

3. The movie was based on a book. The movie was very popular.
   _____
   _____

4. My brother finished reading the long book. My brother loves to read.
   _____
   _____

5. Science fiction makes people consider new ideas. Science fiction makes people dream about the future.
   _____
   _____

Name _____ Date _____

Key Points Reading

"Journey to the Center of the Earth"

Listen as your teacher reads. Follow with your finger.

1. Harry is exploring a gigantic cavern at the center of Earth with his uncle, a professor, and a guide named Hans. They see a large sea, waterfalls, and enormous cliffs. They also find a forest with mushrooms and ferns as tall as trees.

2. The next morning, Harry and his uncle walk along the shore as the high tide rolls in. Harry is surprised that the moon can affect a sea that is 100 miles underground. His uncle, however, is not. He thinks even a subterranean sea should follow the general law of the universe.

3. Harry's uncle wants to cross the sea, so Hans builds a raft. They sail quickly, helped along by the dense atmosphere. As they sail, Harry and Hans fish. Hans catches a small fish which Harry's uncle says has been extinct for many years. Harry worries about what other ancient creatures they might find.

Key Points Reading

"Journey to the Center of the Earth" (continued)

4

Suddenly, a giant sea lizard rises from the water on one side of the raft. Hans steers the raft away from the monster, but a gigantic crocodile appears on the other side. The men reach for weapons, but the creatures attack each other instead of the raft. They fight for hours before disappearing below the water.

5

Safe from the sea creatures, the three explorers sail on. They pass an island with a huge geyser. The clouds above them get darker, and soon the group is caught in a powerful storm. Thunder crashes loudly, and waves toss the little raft.

6

The storm lasts for more than three days and nights. When the raft finally crashes onto land, the explorers believe they have reached the other side of the sea. Then Harry's uncle takes out his compass to check their location. They are not on the other side. The storm tossed them back to the same shore where they started!

Name _____ Date _____

Reread and Retell

"Journey to the Center of the Earth"

Complete the word choice chart with examples from the selection.

Story language	What the words describe	Mood	Impact on reader
"vast, limitless expanse of water"	a large body of water	worried, nervous	The description makes me feel nervous about what will happen in the large, unfamiliar place.

 Complete the chart. Explain to a partner how the author's word choice helped you understand and experience the story. Then have your partner share his or her ideas.

8.20   Unit 8 | Earth and Beyond

Name _____   Date _____

Fluency

"Journey to the Center of the Earth"

Use this passage to practice reading with proper expression.

Looking more closely, I found that he was right. Here were white	12
mushrooms, nearly forty feet high, and with tops of equal size. They	24
grew in countless thousands. The light could not pierce this mushroom	35
forest; beneath them it was dark and gloomy.	43
The gigantic mushrooms were not the only amazing plants at the	54
center of the Earth. New wonders awaited us at every step. Walking a	67
bit farther, we came upon a mighty group of other trees with discolored	80
leaves. They were the common trees of Mother Earth, only many times	92
larger. There were trees a hundred feet high, ferns as tall as pine trees,	106
and gigantic grasses!	109
"Astonishing, magnificent, splendid!" cried my uncle. "Behold the	117
humble plants of our gardens, which in the first ages of the world were	131
mighty trees. Look around you, dear Harry. No botanist ever before	142
gazed on such a sight!"	147

From "Journey to the Center of the Earth," page 281

Expression
- [1] ☐ Does not read with feeling.
- [2] ☐ Reads with some feeling but does not match content.
- [3] ☐ Reads with appropriate feeling for most content.
- [4] ☐ Reads with appropriate feeling for all content.

Accuracy and Rate Formula
Use the formula to measure a reader's accuracy and rate while reading aloud.

_____ − _____ = _____
words attempted   number of errors   words correct per minute
in one minute   (wcpm)

8.21

Name _____ Date _____

Reading Options

"Deep Into Darkness"

Complete the K-W-L-Q chart as you read the science feature.

K What I know	W What I want to know	L What I learned	Q Questions I still have

 Share your questions with a partner. Try to answer the questions together.

Name _____ Date _____

Respond and Extend

Compare Fiction and Nonfiction

Use a comparison chart to compare fiction and nonfiction selections.

	"Journey to the Center of the Earth"	"Deep Into Darkness"
Genre		Nonfiction: Science Feature
Purpose	to entertain	
Structure		
Text features		

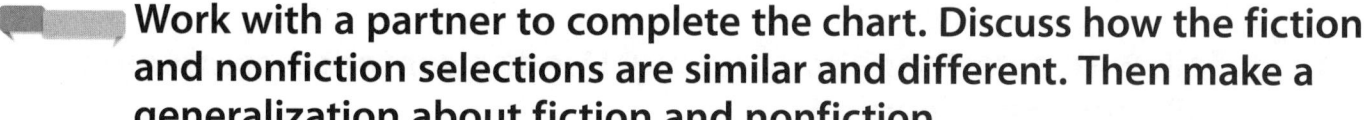 Work with a partner to complete the chart. Discuss how the fiction and nonfiction selections are similar and different. Then make a generalization about fiction and nonfiction.

8.23   Unit 8 | Earth and Beyond

Name _____ Date _____

Grammar

Caves and Cavers

Grammar Rules Combine Sentences

1. Join neighboring sentences or sentences with related ideas.
2. Connect **predicates** about the same subject with **and** or **or**.
3. Join details from two sentences with an **adjective clause**.
4. Connect similar **subjects** with **and** or **or**.

Combine each pair of short sentences into one sentence. Punctuate the new sentence correctly.

1. Cavers wear strong helmets with headlamps. They also use reliable safety harnesses.

   _____

2. Some caves were discovered long ago. Others have been discovered recently.

   _____

3. Caves are special environments. Many amazing animals live in caves.

   _____

4. Cave decorations can take thousands of years to form. Cave decorations can be very fragile.

   _____

5. People can accidentally cause damage. It cannot be undone.

   _____

 Talk with a partner about caving. Use the sentence-combining skills you have learned.

8.24 Unit 8 | Earth and Beyond

Name _____ Date _____

Close Reading

from "Deep Into Darkness," page 297

Analyze the text below with your teacher and make notes.

FROM PEARLS TO POPCORN

1   When minerals dissolve in dripping cave water, they gradually harden into shapes called decorations. Decorations come in many shapes and sizes. Stalactites hang down from a cave ceiling like fangs, and stalagmites poke up from the cave floor. Over time, a stalactite and a stalagmite can meet, grow together, and form a column.

2   Some decorations look like wrinkled stone curtains, and others look like freshly popped kernels of popcorn. Some cave decorations have funny names, like "cave pearls" or "bacon strips." Alvarez has seen formations that look like nests of eggs.

3   Perhaps the most delicate cave formations are called helictites, and you can find them clustered on some cave walls and ceilings. Some clump together like a pile of worms, and others are thicker and look like antlers. One rare type looks like fish tails sticking out of a cave wall! Scientists know a lot about how most cave formations are created, but they still don't know how helictites are formed.

Name _____ Date _____

Close Reading

from "Deep Into Darkness," page 298

Make notes as you read the paragraphs below. Then answer the questions on page 8.27.

CAVE CRITTERS

1. Beautiful cave decorations are not all that you'll see in caves because many animals live or spend time in caves, too. Some animals only visit caves temporarily, while others make caves their homes.

2. Cave-dwelling bats hang out on the walls of caves during the day and go outside to hunt at night. Raccoons, salamanders, lizards, and snakes all use caves as temporary rest areas. Troglobites are animals that live only inside caves, and some live only in one part of one particular cave. Scientists know of about 7,700 kinds of troglobites.

3. Troglobites have adapted to life in the dark. Their skin or shells are pale, and most of them are white. Many of these critters have no eyes because eyes are unnecessary when there is no light. Alvarez has seen eyeless fish, shrimps, and spiders. One type of blind crayfish can live for as many as 175 years!

4. Since they can't see, most troglobites have a super sharp sense of hearing, touch, and smell. A troglobite uses these keen senses for navigation along winding paths and to tell what's nearby.

Name _____ Date _____

Close Reading

from "Deep Into Darkness" (continued)

Reread and annotate the passage to answer these questions.

Reread paragraphs 1–2.

1. Highlight the main idea sentence for this section of the science feature. Explain why it is the main idea.

2. The author says that some animals use caves "temporarily," and some animals "make caves their homes." Highlight evidence in the text that supports these claims.

Reread paragraphs 3–4.

3. Summarize why troglobites are such good hunters. Highlight text evidence that supports your summary.

4. Highlight the heading of this section. Rewrite it in the margin in your own words to give more description.

Name _____ Date _____

Writing Project

Voice

Every writer has a special way of saying things, or a voice. The voice should sound genuine, or real, and be unique to that writer.

	Does the writing sound interesting and unique?	**Does the tone fit the purpose and audience of science fiction?**
4 Wow!	❏ The writing has a unique style and personality. ❏ The writer uses interesting words and phrases and varies the length and types of sentences.	❏ The writer uses precise scientific language and terms. ❏ The details, dialogue, and descriptions appeal to science fiction readers.
3 Ahh.	❏ The writing has a somewhat unique style and personality. ❏ The writer uses some interesting words and phrases and varies some of the sentences.	❏ The writer uses some precise scientific language and terms. ❏ Most details, dialogue, and descriptions appeal to science fiction readers.
2 Hmm.	❏ The writing does not have much style or personality. ❏ The writer uses only a few interesting words and phrases. The sentences do not vary much.	❏ The writer uses some scientific language, but it is not precise. ❏ The details, dialogue, and descriptions do not appeal much to science fiction readers.
1 Huh?	❏ The writing has no style or personality. ❏ The writer does not use interesting words or phrases. The sentences all sound the same.	❏ The writer does not use scientific language. ❏ There is not enough detail, dialogue, or description.

Name _____ Date _____

Writing Project

Plot Diagram

Complete a plot diagram for your science fiction story.

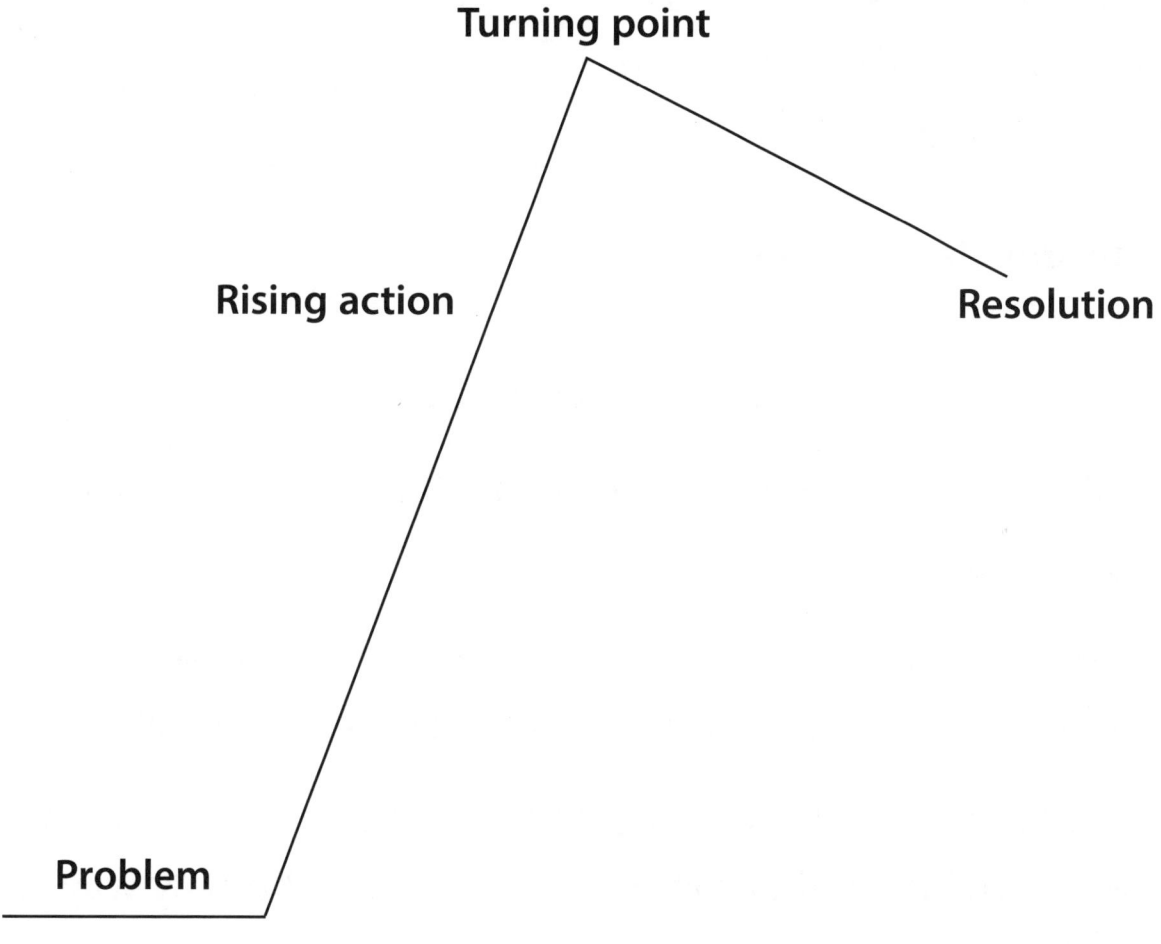

Name ______________________________ Date ____________________

Writing Project

Revise

Use revision marks to make changes to these paragraphs. Look for:

- **places to add dialogue, descriptive details, and precise scientific words**
- **correct organization of plot elements**
- **varied sentence lengths and types**
- **consistent style and tone**
- **places to fix double negatives**

Revision Marks	
^	Add
℘	Take out
⬭⟶^	Move to here
^,	Insert comma
/	Make lowercase

Beware the Asteroid!

The captain stood on the ship's bridge. He didn't think the new asteroid blaster would work.

Finally, the captain said, OK. He didn't have no other choice. The asteroid could hit. It could wipe out the entire planet of Nogula.

Ayla insisted that it would work. Ayla was the Science Commander. She had been working on that thing for years. It was the only way to break up the big asteroid. The asteroid was moving toward Nogula.

Name _____ Date _____

Writing Project

Edit and Proofread

Use revison marks to edit and proofread these paragraphs. Look for:

- incorrect use of punctuation in compound and complex sentences
- run-on sentences
- double negatives
- places where sentences should be combined

Revision Marks	
∧	Add
℘	Take out
∧̓	Insert comma
⊙	Insert period
≡	Capitalize

Beware the Asteroid! (continued)

The captain gave the orders the crew prepared the ship to approach the asteroid.

Ayla took a deep breath. Ayla got behind the controls of the asteroid blaster. The machine had been tested only once before but the ship was within striking distance. Ayla had to act. If she waited any longer to fire the blaster she wouldn't get no other chance. She fired the blaster at the asteroid. Nothing happened!

The captain ordered, "Abort the mission let's get out of here."

"No!" yelled Ayla. She aimed at a different spot. She fired at the asteroid again. This time it worked! a huge chunk of the asteroid floated off into space. Ayla continued firing until the asteroid was no longer a threat.

Photographic Credits

5.4 (t) Spider Martin. (c) Carl Iwasaki/Time & Life Pictures/The LIFE Images Collection/Getty Images. (b) Don Cravens/The LIFE Images Collection/Getty Images. 6.17 (t) dimaberkut/123RF. (c) Ryan McGinnis/Getty Images. (b) Gerd Ludwig/National Geographic Image Collection. 6.18 (t) Micheline Pelletier Decaux/Getty Images. (b) Paul Jeffrey/Alamy Stock Photo. 7.4 (b) Archives Charmet/Bridgeman Images. 7.5 (t) O. Louis Mazzatenta/National Geographic Image Collection. (b) Raga Jose Fuste/Prisma/AGE Fotostock. 8.5 (t) World History Archive/Alamy. (bl) NG Images/Alamy. (br) NASA/Alamy. (t) Science & Society Picture Library/Getty Images.